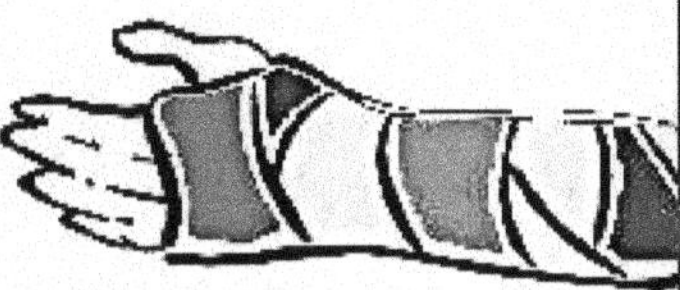

Teconomic Of The Budget Ethics

Hidden Fingers, Invisible Hands, of Free Markets Capitalism

Bahman Fakhraie, PhD

Teconomics of Budget Ethics

Market Organizations and Capitalism
Market Systems Organizations of Capitalism,
Hidden Fingers and Invisible Hands of Free market capitalism

By

Bahman Fakhraie, PhD.

Book- ISBN-10:0989453936
ISBN-13:978-0-9894539-3-6
EBook ISBN-13: 9780989453905
Library of Congress
Copyright case number,
11220155371
$48.85
ISBN 978-0-9894539-3-6
54885>
9 780989 453936

ABSTRACT

This book is an original work about, 'Market Systems Organizations of Capitalism'. A holistic study in 'Teconomics of Market Organizations and Capitalism' requires details of microeconomic components of functional economics systems for policy realignments of economic forces to balance and grow, while resolving macroeconomics issues and imbalances that magnify with data aggregations. That is the microeconomic rigorous mathematical test of optimality, Shepard lemma, and Dr. Bahman Fakhraie additional Sustainability lemmas are reconfirmed at the macro aggregations of data. In the cases, those none-equilibrium game theory balances are applied at micro level, macro aggregate data will show imbalances in the long run.

This study is about some current models, or failed models that have extended outside their relative capacities for well-endued beneficiaries, which have skillfully replaced check and balance and transparencies well organized democracies with tautology of self-interests for mega-international investment banking. Foundational construction will be lasting when it is on good structure, when scientific verifiable and falsifiable tests will assure theoretical soundness, and a secondary evaluation at the aggregate level will show sustainability of balances. The models are tested, which will further illuminate the study subjects. That is grounds for hypothetical rejection exits, if the negative externalities costs are accumulating as societal costs in aggregate data. In this book a simple Popperian test is applied to nominal and real study of aggregate economic data trend lines over the long run economic horizons.

CONTENT

TABLE

Table Page

FIGURES

Figure page

ACKNOWLEDGEMENT

I am thankful to my family for their many ways of being helpful, all errors are mine. I thank my immediate family, Mrs. Kay Davis Fakhraie, Miss Lara F. Fakhraie, Mr. Anayat W. Fakhraie. Special thanks to Dr. S. H. Rokni, world-renowned nuclear physics specialist at Stanford, I thank Professors Lance Girton, Peter W. Philips, Stephen Reynolds, the late professor Ernest William Randa, James Patrick Gander, and J. Steven Ott, I am grateful to Professors E. K. Hunt, Korkut Erturk, David M. Kiefer, Thomas Neil Maloney previous economic department heads. I thank Dr. Khosrow Mostofi , Dr. James Kritzeck, Dr. Hussein Fahim, Haideh Salehi, Robert Edminster, Lawrence Nabors. University of Utah President David W. Pershing, and past president Michael K. Young, Social and Behavioral Sciences Dean M. David Rudd, Graduate school Dean White, Bahman Bakhtiari. I thank friends, professors, and my global family members.

CHAPTER 1

FREE MARKET ORGANIZATIONS

Since the advent of barter, whether tribal, or village-to-village bazars, to modern day garage sales to outdoor markets, or even the more complicated caravans to ocean going ships in big shipyards, and more complicated-global adventures, the exchange of goods have required some degree of organizational complexities.

In the digitized economies exchanges are multibillion exchanges (trades) organized by internet and intranet connectivity globally, between buyers' computers, cell phones, or mobile devices, with the sellers' mobile devices. Therefore, the implications for trade accommodations and job creations are obvious.

The manufactures of market exchanges requires human interventions at different degree of organizational complexities.[1] In case of the suppliers of each modular production process, there is one or a group; therefore, there are supplier organizations. At firm level in economics the classification falls under numerous suppliers, and competitively lower prices. Agricultural smaller modular productions were identified in this competitive free market organizational classification. Even in perfectly competitive free market conditions, sellers, and supplier can join groups, trade unions, sellers' coops to effect pieces of their products higher.

In case of demands for the products or services, there may be individual consumers or tribe, city, or group demands, as buyers' clubs they will reflect the interests in lower costs or prices, (and culture) of the organization with the demand.[2] Nevertheless, individuals can divide the products and consume them individually. An organizational collusion has influenced the exchanges.

Hence, the unusual chance for higher risk events in a group, as part of their organizational behaviors.

The general consensus of classic and neoclassic economists have been that under a theoretical and assumptive perfect market conditions, the economy will balance out equitably and remain sustainable over the long run. The long term is defined about 3-5 years.

The assumptive conditions of free market perfect competition organization are detailed. The mathematical discourses have been extensive.[3] Assumptions are and for of perfect information, or perfect knowledge of prices, wages, interest, costs and rents. The discharges of all supplies and demands in equilibrium prices and wages, etc. will ashore probabilities of continuity of both. The fallacy of composition, in economics states what hold true for the part, must hold true for the whole, or there are consequential longer-term harms.[4] Politically, even in democratic republics, to extend continuities, they may have replaced sustainability, utilizing game theory (as in disequilibrium) instead of assumptive equilibrium conditions. Hence, allowing for different market organizations, other than perfectly competitive market organizations to function in aggregations, and in the longer term, beyond the 5 years periods.

Practitioners in other fields and other economists, econometricians have grown concern that longer-term aggregate data has differed from the happy neoclassical propositions, and scenarios. For example at microeconomic level, wages are held low, and there are full employments at those low wages. Alas, in aggregation, there is not enough aggregate demand and income to sustain market activity. Another example is farmers discover a new technology that will exponentially increase their crops, and they shared it with other farmers. The assumption will be that more output more income. Except, the market organization will reduce price, income, and substantially, if they all stay with that product.

The highest risk events, like criminal activities are not usually clever to disguise for long, while some skims, investment frauds are hidden for some times.

The purely academic exercise of real life events studies the cases that sustainability is upheld, but equilibrium conditions have been waved.

Therefore, especial cases of longer-term damages and harms are studied to show the harmful and extensive effects of negative externality cost, shadow costs, and imbalanced aggregations that can harm the overall economy accumulatively.

INTRODUCTION

There may be false assumptions that economic hypothesis are not tested, or they are not testable, so anything goes. In this book a simple Popperian test is applied to nominal and real study of aggregate economic data. Since, subject attracted research, and this methodology was applied in mid 1970s, the result and conclusions have become more cemented. Therefore, the experience is shared with student of economic and political economics, to save the public from the negative consequences. Policies advance on unsound intellectual foundations, gather negative externalities, and social costs, regardless of good or patriotic intentions of the political sources of those policies. If the original intentions are negative, these policies venture into unethical teconomics hinterlands.

Hidden Fingers, Invisible Hands, Markets

Hidden fingers, invisible hands, and free markets assumed false idols status outside their academic paradigms. Hidden fingers, invisible hands, and assumptive perfectly competitive free markets have come up short in estimations of the crowds, now. Theologically, supply-siders, marketers, and student-economists were admonished to avoid market-money worship, as idolatry. Aside from a prayer for less inflated commodities prices and more inflated wages and salaries, do economics or social sciences have anything to illuminate in their field, philosophically or scientifically?

Since perfectly competitive markets are only hypothetical in capitalism, there are hidden hands in free markets, which cause negative externalities (shadow costs) to increase. These negative externalities, costs become astronomical in markets for goods and services with calculated inelastic demands and with the none-competitive organization power players, without the check and balance of the promised invisible hands. There are the Adam Smith invisible hand incentives, which added profit for entrepreneurial sprits, operational profits to small farms, livable wages to motivate workers, and value to products, and it is included in the costs of each item honestly, within his moral frameworks. Besides, the difficulties about prefect knowledge and competitions in real markets, some social scientists seem to ignore the assumptive conditions that Adam Smith established in his two books, and go for the easy steps, as I discovered in1970s.

There are world of difference between the two free markets capitalism-scenarios, this escapes the intellectual grasp of many amateur politicians, and student-economists. These at micro abstracts seem small; however, in dynamic macroeconomics, with the technological injections steroids, add up to be harmful to individuals and national budgets.

There were good sad examples at the start of this week. They are all over the media, but there are more examples, which they never see daylights, or media attention.

The first example is the negative externalities, of United States, football-games brain injuries, in the multibillion-dollar industry that affects lot of younger

American lives, and it is equal parts, Apple pie, the flag, and Americana.

The hidden parts are enumerable in older ball players that fade and die in the darker corners of American anonymities, their families and younger ball players may have their career and future ended with cheers and dancing angles with pompoms bursting in the air around their heads, with permanent bodily injuries, and career ending disabilities. Perfect knowledge, information honestly shared will help the decision-making somewhat. If we let everyone and their moms know the costs and negative externalities upfront, the music may not stop, but the accounting may change, and society will get enough to pay for the brokenness left in the trail of this glory.

So far, only the families, American taxpayers, and small communities have internalized the costs, and the harsh lumps of life that came with those hidden hands. Perhaps, that is no longer possible.

Damaged Bodies, Brains, and Reputations

Can free market fix brokenness, it does not see. The information and facts can be hidden from the markets, intentionally, criminally, or ignorantly. A physician discovers CTE in the donated brain tissue of a late great football player Mike Webster, applying well-established traditional medical science.[5] There are long trails of damaged bodies, brains, and reputations left in the way to causation-linkage of CTE/brain damage and playing football.

In pro-players, when doctors were tested donated brains, the probabilities in at least two samples were 95 percent, and 97 percent. Watching boxers and fighters, the arguments and accepting the causation-linkage proposition had been around.

The new studies will become more conclusive, because brain-imaging technologies have advanced the pool of victims from the dead pro-players, to living victims' brain scans, like the high school and college players, and dropout-football players of all ages.

However, up to now, the new samples and tests have increased the probabilities of causation-linkage of CTE/brain damage and playing football, and the tests have not reduced them, that the causation-linkage of CTE/brain damage and playing football is stronger hypotheses now than before.[6]

There is a legal settlement for retired pro-players a laudable giant leap financially, but somehow the size of negative externalities and shadow costs of the games and lives of the younger players may never be recognized. There are series of PBS/frontline reports that have kept up with some of these lives and the subject, which is good journalism.[7]

The full sacrifices of all, before we arrive at this moment of Super Ball entertainment climax is a dynamic that will continue after the games, and after retirement of these great players, and with their families, and children. One way to mitigate these lives is to establish funds to cover the damages of all involved, at high schools and colleges levels, too.

It will be greater for the games to do well in business ethics and for graceful sportsmanship to step over the greed, to acknowledge the full sacrifices of other people in this game of multi-billion dollars entertainments, so we can conceivably keep the games, and we can probably all be winners in the longer run.

Nevertheless, now we all know before we play, what are the full costs and the nature of this great game, to children and younger players, to our hero pro-players, to their family members, to an honorable society that will have to pick up the brokenness.

You can decide if a caveat emptor can do all these cases justice, or a set-aside fund is needed, may be government (tax and benefits) can do it, in these oceans of deceit, hidden fingers, megalomaniacal profiteering, and legal obstructionisms, organizational self-benefiting. Some entities need to guarantee that multimillion-dollar players as well younger-players have a chance at a living, if the worst happens to them.

The shut-down-government politics have in-house polemicists defeating their cases regularly, because hidden fingers of criminal conducts, dishonesties, and xenophobic, bigoted, sexists' ignorance undermine their arguments for good government.

Drug Wars, Drug-Legalization, Criminal Hidden Hands

What age of inhumanity thunders?
Wonderments and conundrums aplenty,
Opiates are well rewarding, and deadly to all innocence,
Wisdom is life giving, and punishingly unrewarded.[8]

Other hidden costs will need sunlight, too. The negative externalities of drug wars, one on hard drugs (heroin, meth, cocaine) that fail, and we have young victims self-destroying themselves. Another one that was a waste of rare resources, and it will become an inelastic commodity (marijuana, Alcohol, tobacco), but still there will be victims like with the alcoholic road-kills and health problems, and tobacco cancerous sagas, on daily or nightly news, an at familial atomistic budget bases.

There are victims with high sugar, fat, and salt content processed food, when lab-tested manufactured food has replaced fresh food, combined with sedentary low-income life style of most Americans, and all others that join in the American life style, globally.

What is astonishingly irresponsible is that certain state governments blame these issues on the immigrants (or illegals) less than 0.033 percent of the population.

They have managed to parley these types of xenophobic unintellectual legalese into profiling reports full of index-illusions (biases), public policies, illegal immigrant profiling, self- deportations, administrative removals. Legal immigrants do not fear much better, multiple delays, blocks, and increasing fees toward citizenships' process of even legal immigrants and foreign-born American citizens, which are only 14 percent of the total population. The true American natives, in USA and Alaska, the indigenous American people there are 5.3 million, only 2 percent of the population. American citizens that they called 'native' with criminal records are estimated at 20 percent of population.

DHS yearbook data statistic show 267 percent higher total removal versus the criminal alien removal.[9] Moreover, USA BAR had issued a warning on treatment and procedurals.[10] Some of immigration judges themselves have complained about lack of legal representation, luck of translators, and alarming disparities of results among different judges and jurisdictions, thus red-flagging the inadequacy of the process.

It is understandable that infusion of cash brings results and a lot of big technologies, the quality of the result is another issues, and who, what, and how the wheels of the machinery grinds used to matter the American democracy, judiciary, and Justices in less prejudice times.

> "(US-VISIT) program surpassed $17.9 billion in fiscal year (FY) 2012. This amount is nearly 15 times the spending level of the US Immigration and Naturalization Service (INS)"
>
> And,
>
> "In the ensuing 26 years, the nation has spent ($219.1 billion if adjusted to 2012 dollars) on immigration enforcement by INS and its successor agencies, CBP and ICE, and the US_VISIT program."[11]

Nevertheless, the anti-immigration laws propose transfer of resources from fighting the hard drug crimes, and apply them to immigrations policing, instead of the real issues.

Therefore, they are ham-hogging efficient commerce, and good policing, for modern day emotionalism and bad-labeling conservatism, in ignorance. National resources can be preoccupies with violations of three hundred million people citizens-constitutional rights.

The misapplications of resources can enrage at least around 2 billion Muslims worldwide, and alienate and insult 7 billion potential cell-phones-customers globally, pre-emptively as probable terrorists, while less than 3000 or 300 people harbor ill-intends, and they are probably organized to carry it out, from known areas.

Making it even harder to identify or distinguish bad people from good. Nevertheless, we can increase the poll of dead-end makers by irresponsible intolerances, general warrants, and abuse by head cracking police squads domestically and internationally.[12] United States of all nations have had the most vivid experiences of civil right social unrest under most abusive misuse of police force. It is very difficult to argue bigoted ill-intends and xenophobic mischiefs are not behind repetition of that particular history, and which institutions' hands are clean.

All these examples needed better (more efficient) federal governmental involvements, than jailhouse jubilees and monetization theatrics in extremists' states.

Especially if xenophobia, discriminations, racial profiling, lazy or militarists' police-works pollute the data samples from states to states, which it will waste resources, and leave capitals and personals preoccupied with the wrong endeavors, while the hard drugs kill more people faster.

Aside from the more frequent recent videos of police illegal shootings at family vans, frequently deadly or improper use of Tasers, states have tampered with the evidences and DNA, charged, and executed innocent people, usually minorities with an alarming higher frequency.

Therefore, it is unusually alarming to hear states push both to militarize their police forces, and they want them to enforce immigration federal laws. Since, the classified hard drugs have such expansion of their supplies nationwide, and the body counts to confirm it. It is important to see where the concentration of resources, which is police work and money to hire police persons, can be realigned.

THE GLOBAL INSECURITY AGENDAS

More experienced politicians are recalculating the economics of rare resource utilization and applications by making distinctions between true national security, and wasteful and harmful constitutional violations for monetizing and insiders' revolving doors agendas, and newer industrial complexes. Just how many billions in costs of negative externalities the nation would like to endure? How many international businesses and contracts will be lost with vanishing global trusts, internet data tribalism, World Wide Web security honeycombs, retaliatory demonization, and diminution of international trade and commerce?

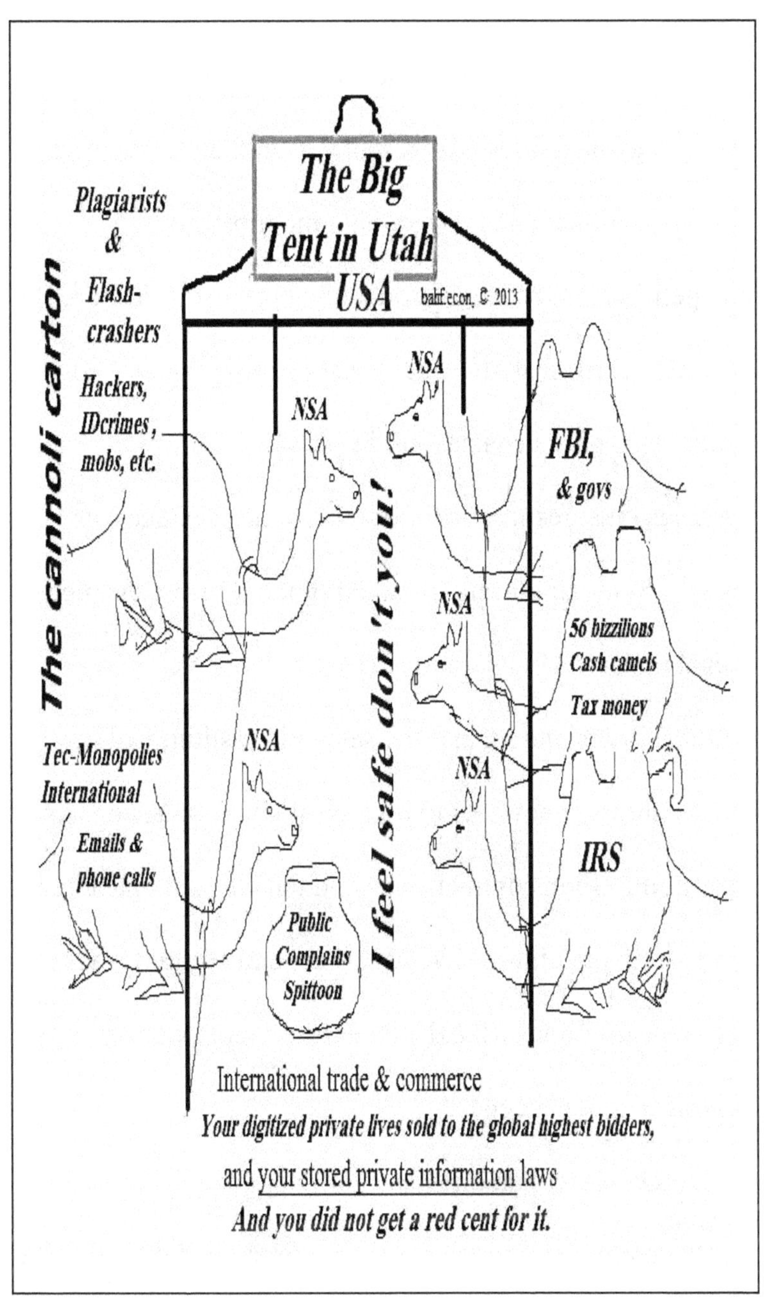
The Big
Tent in Utah
USA
bahf.econ, © 2013
The cannoli carton
Plagiarists
&
Flash-
crashers
Hackers,
IDcrimes,
mobs, etc.
Tec-Monopolies
International
Emails &
phone calls
NSA
NSA
NSA
NSA
NSA
I feel safe don't you!
FBI,
& govs
56 bizzilions
Cash camels
Tax money
IRS
Public
Complains
Spittoon
International trade & commerce
Your digitized private lives sold to the global highest bidders,
and your stored private information laws
And you did not get a red cent for it.

What damages will the United States enfant-technology industries will sustain? Can they survive the wave of national and international monopsony-competitions in the same product markets? In addition, how much will that affect sectorial unemployment? The actual walk backs enacted are important.[13] However, the agencies must respect or follow the actual practices, or laws.[14] Some of current divulged practices were deemed illegal under TALON, in the 2000s.[15] However, new political organization, and the same old institutional actors means, they get newbies to do their illegal deeds, and keep their multibillion contracts, or bend the laws, or enact new unconstitutional laws. The use of general warrants, have been constitutionally band, since the red coat war of American independence.

On more than one occasions, agencies have pushed for that en mass criminalization, phone-meta data and USA national license-plate data warehousing (private or government) are the just latest skinny-dipping in the muddy waters.[16] Why and when did that become such a herculean efforts? At least by now, the complexities of <PATRIOTs ACTs> sunsets-requirements have enlightened the civilian honest monitors.[17] The answers are another wonderment of modern American politics.

It is only recently, the revolving door natures of intelligence super-duper financial constructs were exposed. The hand-offs and the hand-downs, and revolving doors, accommodative laws leave nothing to the imagination. When did middle class and poor American taxpayers replace foreign terrorists and drug lords on the lists? On the other hand, were those the original clever-job-creation plans of the forever wars? How much money was transferred from domestic infrastructures job-creations into the crocodile funds? Did our civilian representatives' monitors (house and senate) ever ask any hard questions? Moreover, why do you think they are trying very hard to stop your votes for 2014, 2016? Because Mr. and Mrs. America it is your votes that will stop the wrongs. The votes will induce the pushbacks, the checks, and the balances of democracy.

NOTE

[1] Thus, groups form around certain market causes.

[2] For a great discussion and new scholarly look at organizational culture read this book.
J. Steven Ott, *The Organizational Culture Perspective*, California Pacific Grove, Brook/Cole Publishing Co., 1989

[3] Dr. Bahman Fakhraie's books 'Teconmics" and more recent books have detailed the mathematic formulations for equilibrium and sustainability conditions.

[4] Professor Paul Anthony Samuelson, and William Samuelson, *Economics*, 11th Ed., New York, McGraw-Hill Book Company, 1980, Pp.,11, 663

[5] "Growing up in Nigeria, Dr. Bennet Omalu knew next to nothing about American football. He did not watch the games, he did not know the teams, and he certainly did not know the name Mike Webster"
Jason M. Breslow, The Autopsy That Changed Football, October 6, 2013, 8:06 am ET
http://www.pbs.org/wgbh/pages/frontline/sports/league-of-denial/the-autopsy-that-changed-football/

[6] Steve Fainaru and Mark Fainaru-Wada, New Study Finds Brain Damage in Living Ex-NFL Players, January 22, 2013, 2:09 pm ET
http://www.pbs.org/wgbh/pages/frontline/sports/concussion-watch/new-study-finds-brain-damage-in-living-ex-nfl-players/

[7] http://www.pbs.org/wgbh/pages/frontline/league-of-denial/

[8] Dr. Bahman Fakhraie © 2/2/2014

[9] Doris Meissner, Donald M. Kerwin, Muzaffar Chishti, and Claire Bergeron, "Immigration Enforcement in the United States: The rise of a Formidable Machinery," Washington D.C., Migration policy institute, 2013, 119

[10] Arnold & Porter LLP, "reforming the Immigration System: proposal to promote Independence, Fairness, Efficiency, and Professionalism in Adjudication of Removal cases," American Bar Association Commission on Immigration, granted permission for copy, 2010 http://www.americanbar.org/content/dam/aba/publications/commission_on_immigration/coi_complete_full_report.authcheckdam.pdf
and
http://www.americanbar.org/news/abanews/aba-news-archives/2013/08/know_your_rights.html

[11] Doris Meissner, Donald M. Kerwin, Muzaffar Chishti, and Claire Bergeron, "Immigration Enforcement in the United States: The rise of a Formidable Machinery," Washington D.C., Migration policy institute, 2013

[12] By H. Gude, M.Popp, J. Schindler, and F. Schmid, Translated from the German by Thomas Rogers SPIEGEL Staff, Right-Wing Extremism Germany's New Islamophobia Boom, Spiegel, 03/05/2014 05:02 PM

URL:http://www.spiegel.de/international/germany/islamophobic-hate-groups-become-more-prominent-in-germany-a-956801-druck.html

[13] Remarks by the President on Review of Signals Intelligence
January 17, 2014, available at
www.whitehouse.gov
Liberty and Security in a Changing World: Report and Recommendations of the President's Review Group on Intelligence and Communications Technologies
December 12, 2013, 303 pp., available at
www.whitehouse.gov

[14] David Cole, Can Privacy Be Saved?
http://www.nybooks.com/articles/archives/2014/mar/06/can-privacy-be-saved/?pagination=false

[15] By Marcel Rosenbach, Laura Poitras and Holger Stark, How the NSA Accesses Smartphone Data, Spiegel,
http://www.spiegel.de/international/world/how-the-nsa-spies-on-smartphones-including-the-blackberry-a-921161.html

[16] "The Central Intelligence Agency's attempt to keep secret the details of a defunct detention and interrogation program has escalated a battle between the agency and members of Congress and led to an investigation by the C.I.A.'s internal watchdog into the conduct of agency employees."
By MARK MAZZETTIMARCH, C.I.A. Employees Face New Inquiry Amid Clashes on Detention Program, 4, 2014

http://www.nytimes.com/2014/03/05/us/new-inquiry-into-cia-employees-amid-clashes-over-interrogation-program.html?_r=3U.S.

[17] Report on the Telephone Records Program Conducted under Section 215 of the USA PATRIOT Act and on the Operations of the Foreign Intelligence Surveillance Court by the Privacy and Civil Liberties Oversight Board January 23, 2014, 234 pp., available at www.fas.org, and http://www.itep.org/whopays/

CHAPTER 2

COMPETITIVE ORGANIZATIONS

Competitive market organization, in the case of suppliers of each modular production process, there is one or a group trying to sell their goods or services. Therefore, there are supplier organizations. In the case of demands for the products or services, there may be individual consumers or tribes, city, or groups' demand, which will be reflected in an organization with the demand.[1] The minimum potential originations for perfectly competitive exchanges are at least three.

The supplier, the consumer, and the exchange market are three elements of each exchange, which is accomplished by a buyer and a seller, and the buyer can be the modular producer. Therefore, there are potential for at least two market organizations in a perfectly competitive market.

THE SUPPLY-SIDERS' MODELS FAILED DATA TESTS,

There has always been a diaspora between the ultra-wealthy and the rest of the economy, it is widening exponentially, while national structural unemployment has stayed high long after the recent economic recovery post-recession. The demagogues love to argue 'eat-the rich', Socialism, Marxism slogans in defense or offense. The gathering clouds of discontents far more important than their collective and limited vocabulary, at this time in history of aging modern technology-capitalism.

There are the violations of assumptive conditions, formulated by the perfectly competitive market models, which I presented as rarities in 1970s, they have become more pronounced in millennial economies. Then there are the more realistic models, of relative free markets, and natural or governmental oligopolies and monopolies. These form , the all shades of gray that is imperfect competition models, and more complex organizational involvements in multinational markets, which have gathered momentum, aggregate macroeconomics forces, and they affect policy, and sustainability conditions readily (you may have to read my first two books for more serious details).

In discussion of income inequalities, poverty, and dynamic models of wealth creation within the relatively free market models of capitalism it is very important to study the longer run implications of micro and macroeconomic balances and economic welfare theory. Economic-theorists may recall Joan Robinson (Cambridge, UK.), and Dr. Edward H. Chamberlin (Harvard, USA), '1933' to 1980s Microeconomic discourse, if they need to refresh their older theories. I had a short visit with Mrs. Robinson in late 1970s, early 1980.

Hence, the reason for democratic governments' attentions to the sustainability balances of wealth-creation, as a counter balance force to self-harm of raw-wealth and unchecked-political power concentrations, in political monopolistic capitalism.[2]

Therefore, sound fiscal policies are not some demagogic loyalty oath to memory of Carl Marx, despite the anti-socialism cacophony of the millionaire media crowds. Recently, wealthy capitalists (nouveau riche) have realized their toolboxes of purchased political powers. They have used it too excessively. Nevertheless, they have not all realized their responsibilities, and the steroidal effects of technological injections, thus the consequential imbalances. Therefore, they have ignored the backlash powers, which are accumulative and unleash unexpectedly.

There are educated capitalists some old school, "let pay our share of taxes crowds (plus a minimum cooperate tax), for education, infrastructural, and reparative fiscal job-creation, so the economy uplifts all yachts and kayaks."

They also realized the government rule as a counterbalance to the negative forces that cause class poverties, as a force for sustainability instead of poverty creation at one extreme, and wealth creation at another, and accumulative forces of social Darwinism. The purchased gradual drift from the hard educations of 1930s history have harvested both momentum and claw backs.

We can name many of the one percent wealthy that are wise beyond their billions. They contribute to global health and welfares infrastructure immensely, by self-governing, self-motivational, and very effectually. They have greatly reduced global infant mortality rate. They have supplemented or supported willing local governments. They have supplemented commercial enterprises, and created many jobs, and their own eminence wealth, all laudable endeavors for detractors and admirers. Their wealth creation will not be problematic to job-creation, or to national wealth creation strategies.

However, the rate of zero-sum-game version of wealth concentrations, and its implications, its hostility to others livable wages, level of livings, direct impact on aggregate demand, economic activates, circularity and velocity of money in national and international economy are consequential accumulatively. They are massively influencing economic policies, political-policy. Their effort will affect employment, taxation, and rRDIPPC. These make them, their method of wealth concentration central to economic solutions, just by paying a reasonable tax rate, nothing confiscatory, as they fear initially. Histories tell of accumulative pent-up forces, which are not too kind to capital constructionists that dillydallied too long.

The immense diversion of incomes will meet the usual spin and forget treatment from the media. However, the exploding diversions have explosive social instabilities issues.

The usual spin-jobs or the one-party political maneuvering and push for re-election funds will not serve the systems well. The expansive issues of the American people and the need of educated wealthy patrons are not good justification for them to depart from their honestly earned hard cash, if all they get is none-functionality and hostile environments to commerce locally or globally.

Legacy Benefits of Cooperate citizens

The cooperation of the market organizations of the top one percent brackets for individuals and cooperate entities are reflected in their rate of economic benefits, which they are amassing at exponential rates to top one percent organizational groups.

The progress of all income and economic activates for all quintiles hide the fact that middle-income earners decreased, or their earnings remained flat, as their costs are, (COLA) inflated. That is the fallacy of index-illusions of economic, when a small number get large incomes, and large numbers get very little, the averages can falsely show a large average income for the sample population. We will see the important implications of wealth concentration instead of wealth creation as national policies.

Figure 1 shows top one percent and all other quintiles' income earners incomes, before and after taxes in United States, 1979-2010.

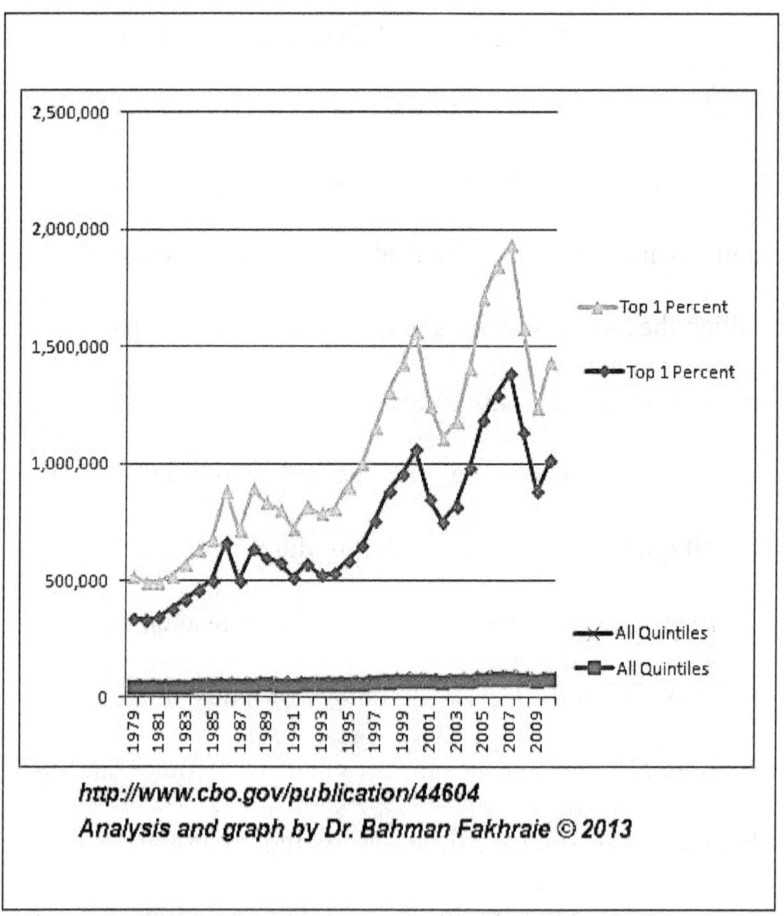

Figure 1, Top 1 % and other quintiles' incomes, before and after taxes.

The next two graphs show the cooperation's' wealth concentration that have followed the Supreme Court pro-cooperate, citizen decisions in USA. Figure 2, shows income paid that has increase, for cooperation interests in Untied States in 2002-2010.[3]

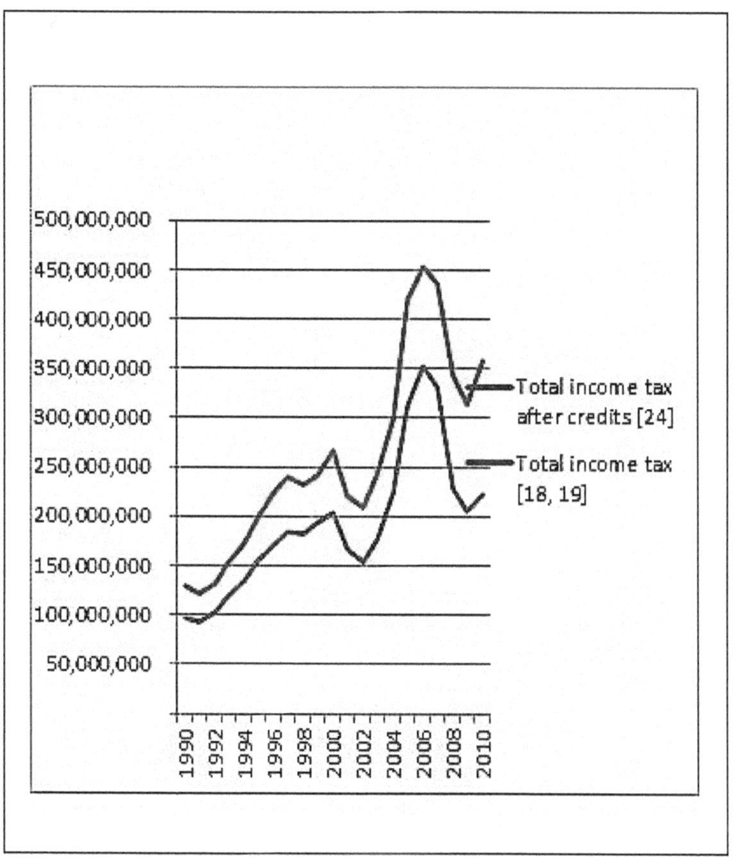

Figure 2, Cooperation income taxes data.

The good top 1 percent citizens even carry out infrastructural duties, when governments fail. The late industrialists' Henry Ford and the advocacy of late Senator Teddy Kennedy are vivid examples. Figure 3 shows cooperation profits and net income that have exploded in Untied States in 2002-2010.[4]

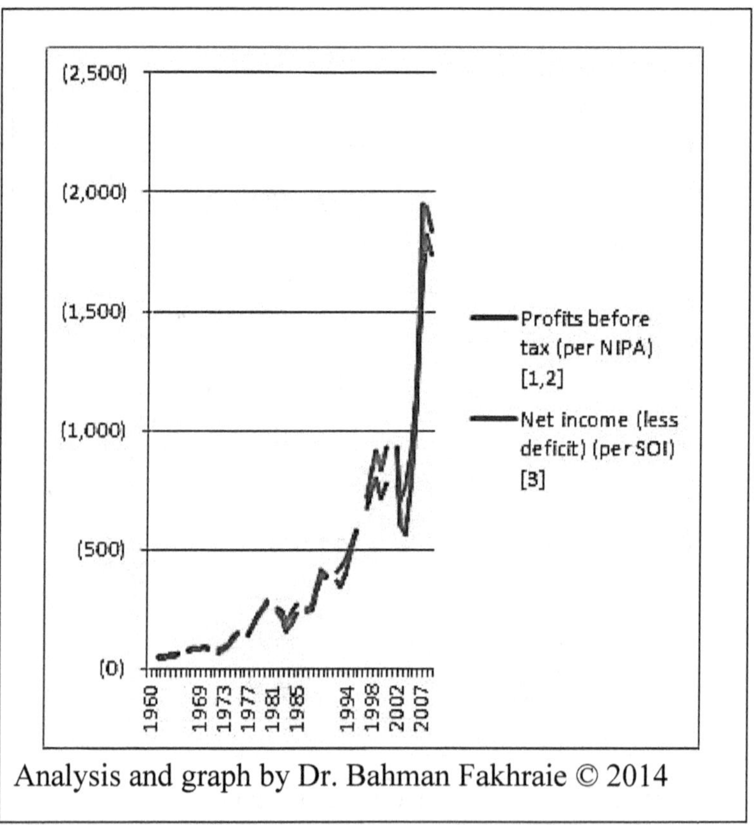

Analysis and graph by Dr. Bahman Fakhraie © 2014

Figure 3, Cooperation net incomes, and profits.

However, there are the uneducated nouveau riche capitalists, or more deliberate capitalists' mega rich. They carry politics and spins full of rhythmic bull, which means. What is mine is mine, what is the middle class and poor is mine, too.

> 'The let them eat cake kinds, they need to pull up their own bootstraps. Tax the middle class takers, not the wealthy job makers.'

Unfortunately, they are not the job-makers. They are deporting (self-deporting) the job-makers. Nevertheless, they purchase cash-hoarding wealth-concentrating policies. These policies nourish certain lower skilled practitioners, and none-functionality that adds to the accumulated negative externalities and unsustainability forces that histories tell us, they are very destabilizing. While the funds of the workers, and middle class pension savers, the elderly savings remain in the country and are recycled as consumer demands and up to 75 to 78 percent of GDP, and as producers- investments in real estate and job-creations domestically.

However, the transfer of government tax for revenues have shifted to individuals, to older workers that are retiring and need healthcare, Medicare, social security, and pension protection laws, and geriatric care, as the RDI declines, so will the economy decline. So does their pension, IRAs, and saving.

These legacy benefits are regularly under verbal attacks by the worst of the worst of cooperate criminals, riders, and their high salaried financial media minions. Their spins are against the rich elderlies, and the CEOs, the multibillionaires, the hedge funders, with the $ 300 million to billion dollars salaries, bonuses, and benefits get the media pass, and the rare admiration nibble. It is all fine, if they pay their minimum cooperate tax rate.

The CEOs have driven cooperation their operations overseas to monetize their productions (modular productions) for higher CEOs salaries and benefits. They hire the best professionals to under pay or not pay taxes. The top one percent pays less than 10 percent of taxes. They have avoided the flat minimum cooperate tax rate of 30 percent under the last three presidents, and both parties, and in both houses.

They are also wrecking immigration policies since President Reagan. In order to reduce competitions with their organizational operations in foreign-markets, where they can hire American university educated skilled workers, deported from America and American universities on the cheap.

The same graduates they denigrate as unskilled at home in USA, while equating and blaming unemployment on immigrants, they are deporting the job makers, too. The last two graphs showed their explosive revenue growth. There have not been any sufficient job creations or RDI increases to benefit the government revenue or aggregate demands, domestically.

The job-creations promised by both parties for large groups among the middle class have not appeared. The lack of a fixed immigration policy harms the elderly GOP most, since their pensions are deemed removable by the CEOs and the GOP politicians as bad legacy costs, too. Why would any honest American President buy their oppositions political lines and keep deporting Americans at thousand a day rates?

Figure 4 shows the reduction of cooperation taxes per total assets. That is 50 percent drop in cooperate tax obligations since 1995, 17 percent decline 1995-2006, and an additional 33 percent decline 2006-2010. This is at the same time that the middle class tax breaks were terminated during 2013 tax years.

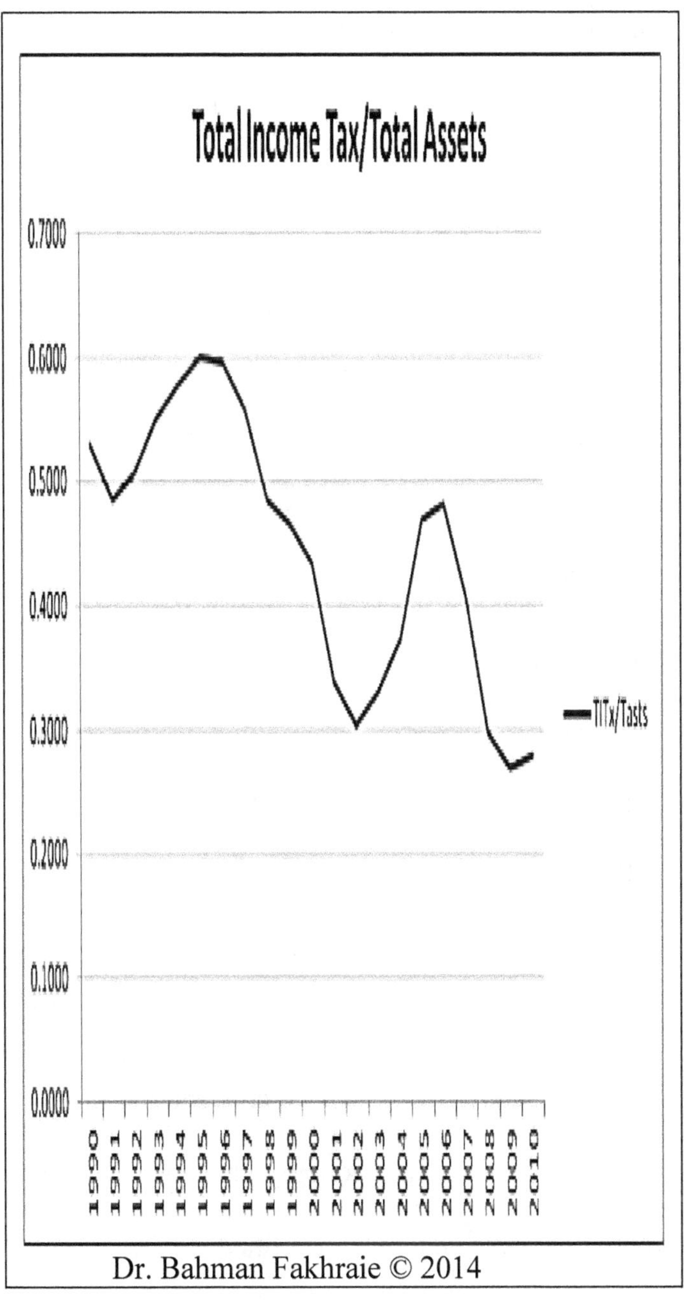

Dr. Bahman Fakhraie © 2014

Figure 4, Total income tax over total assets for cooperation data.

It is difficult to accept the argument that only criminal elements are deported, while summary judgments and court cases have been reported as one-a-minute judgments. Indeed, these are their expressed-observed facts. Moreover, we have a history of general warrants against select population. In addition, The history of summery rash judgments against big groups, nationalities, colors, sexes, tribal nations, whether they are Asian, Chinese, Japanese, American Indians, or Muslims, Jews, sick, and others. This has only recently improved marginally, under intense scrutiny and vigilance of a great American public. Less we forget our vigilance, bad things in history reoccur.

Figure 5, shows while wealth concentration have been in the one sector of the economy, the upper brackets tax revenues has declined, like it declined for the cooperation interests in aggregation.

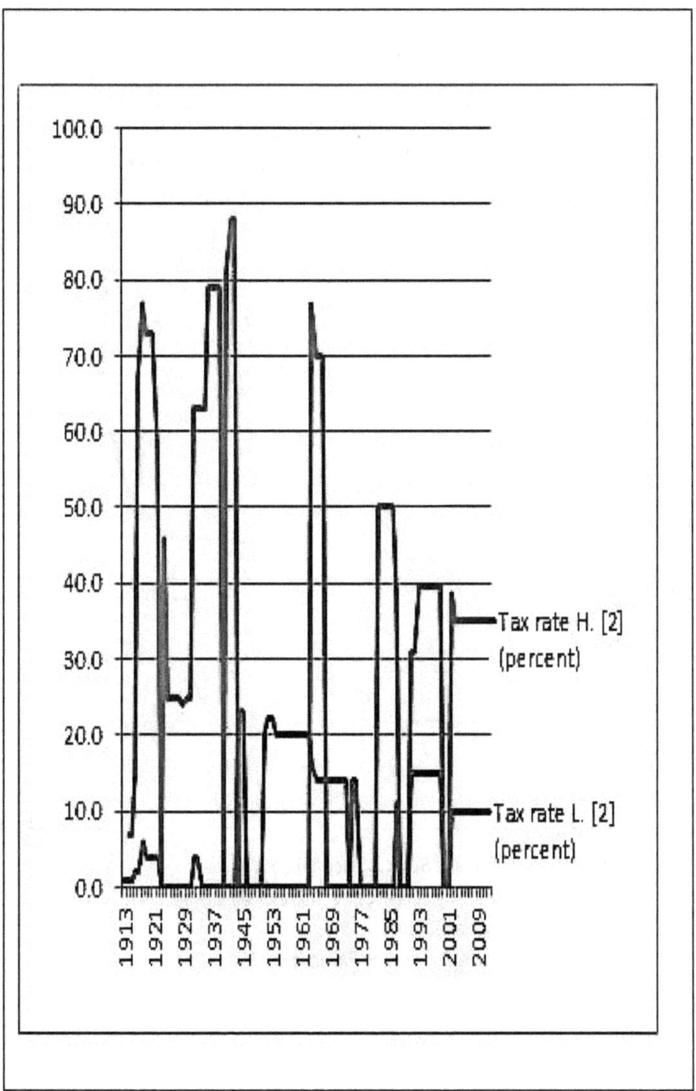

Figure 5, highest and lowest tax brackets tax rates 1913-2009.

Figure 6 shows federal revenues from selected major tax-sources.

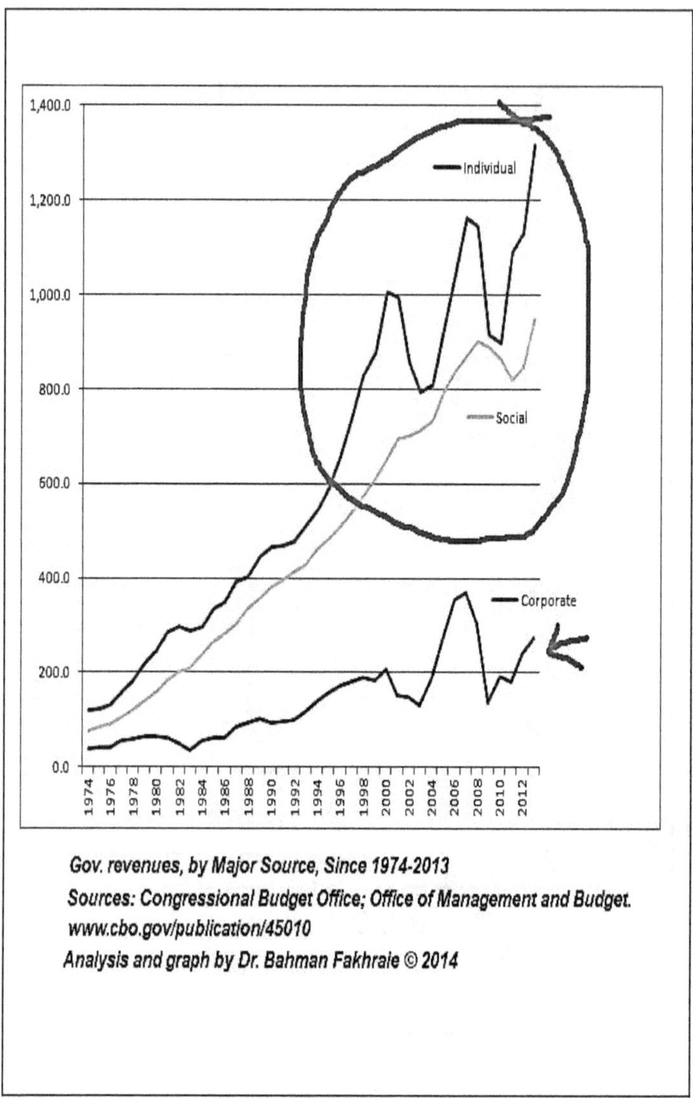

Gov. revenues, by Major Source, Since 1974-2013
Sources: Congressional Budget Office; Office of Management and Budget.
www.cbo.gov/publication/45010
Analysis and graph by Dr. Bahman Fakhraie © 2014

Figure 6, Federal revenues from selected major tax-sources.

Figure 6 shows that it took 80-90 percent taxes rates 1920s to1940s, it may take 30 percent cooperate-minimum flat tax now to repair their harms. Even optimistically, it will take 40 percent later, and 55 percent by 2025 to repair their damages, if these jobless-recoveries remain as our economic norms. They are hoping their organizational control of the political machinery and both parties will suffice to get those taxes from the middle class and working poor. That reality may prove much harsher.

Tax Burden Shift and Decision Matrix

History tells a different story, 1920s their firm grasps of mantels of power was much firmer than it is now, Hoovers' supply-siders were serious about their remedies, and they were resolute adamantly. Yet, they had to pay up to 90 percent in taxes to repair the damages to the societal infrastructure, structural implosions, and resuscitation of the employments systems. Even if their political control nightmare scenario is succeeding now, the money, the cash flow, based on the trends of RDI, and their inabilities to create jobs, or pass a job creation bill will not generate revenue from (declining population of) individual taxpayers to compensate this historic cooperate ride on the treasury.

This has occurred with the blessing of their representatives in both political party, but mainly by the GOP. Everyone needs to recalculate the balance of his or her greed with the functionality in the economic system anew, in a way that improves others economic condition as well.

Those obstruction-mindsets cause paranoiac policies, against everyone except the one percent, which causes backlash. Their represented media, and journals, their purchased-political monopolistic spins and attack-machines push these policies for the failed supply-siders. They push the "Nazis-Kristallnacht" economic-models not objective news, or sciences.[5] Therefore, their ignorance is harmful to national security, beyond intentional harming of a black president and his legacy agenda, or legal immigrants, or middle class economics. Moreover, it will cost more to fix their damages to the economy. Figure 7 shows Federal revenues major sources as percentage of gross national products (GDP, 1974-2013).

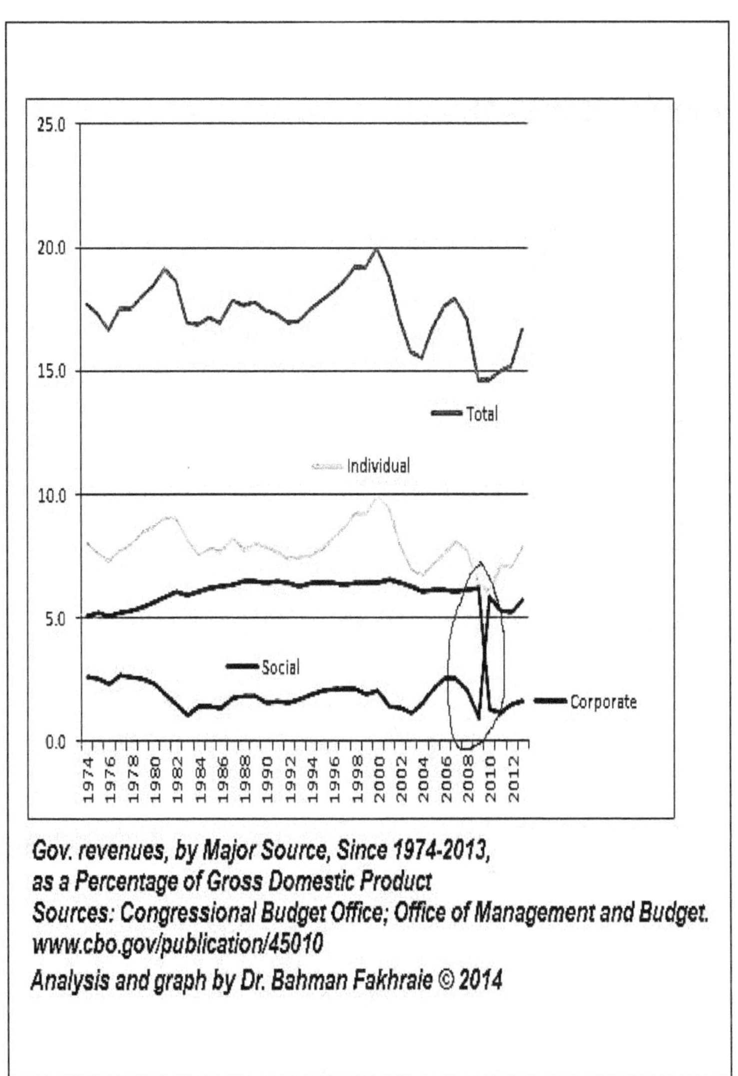

Gov. revenues, by Major Source, Since 1974-2013, as a Percentage of Gross Domestic Product
Sources: Congressional Budget Office; Office of Management and Budget. www.cbo.gov/publication/45010
Analysis and graph by Dr. Bahman Fakhraie © 2014

Figure 7, Federal revenues as percentage of GDP, 1974-2013.

Cooperation taxes have dropped already, the average-cooperation tax rate as a percentage of GDP has dropped from 6.5 percent (averages until 2009) to 1.4 percent, (averages 2010-2013).[6] The policy upgrades are not just for moral or ethical fortitudes, since they are needed badly. Because their political agendas is too destabilizing to the sustainability conditions of the free enterprise capitalist market systems, which have proven to be most productive for their interests above everyone else in the society. If they really succeed in harming it, other alternative systems, cultures, or countries will deal with their interests much more harshly, than American democracy.

Therefore, it is important to fix the system in a way to benefit everyone's' economic future, and societal wellbeing. Robbing Peter to cheat Paul will have lasting consequential impacts on social welfare equilibriums. It will derail economic sustainability. It is a poorer political economic choice.

Table 1 shows a decision matrix, formulated in percentages from average taxes of individual income taxes and their social benefit taxes overtime and average of cooperate taxes over time and over total taxes, 1974-2013.

This table 1, tax shift matrix shows a tax burden shuffle from cooperation to individual taxes and social benefit taxes of individuals. This reconfirms, what figure 4, and figure 7 represented about the taxes. That cooperate taxes per total cooperate assets have declined. The upper bracket taxes have also declined. Only taxes for the lower brackets have increased.

Table 1, Tax shifts in matrix percentages, USA 1974-2013.

Matrix of Tax Shifts, as Percant of GDP		
Avgs/yrs	Individual & Social Taxes	Cooperate Taxes
1974-09	**57**	**35**
2009-13	**82**	**9**

Nevertheless, there is an attempt made to shift all of the economic burdens to middle class and working poor, without giving them an income increase that matched COLA, or regular raises.

There has been a lot of political money paid to arrange elections, and hide this simple tax shuffle among other agendas. Most of government revenues are collected from the individual income taxes with flat or declining DPI. In the worst case of hiding the trick-hands, the right wing media have attacked the democratic administration for IRS tax targeting of the wealthy and c-nonprofits, while the big news is the need for a minimum-cooperation-tax rate, and the tax loud shuffle to the middle class 47 percent, and the other 99 percent.

Yet, we see the opposite is true by the USA aggregate data that it is the middle class and working poor have been burdened for cost of government, while tax burden has been shifted away from the cooperation and the mega wealthy, for the fake promise of job-creations. The promised they signed in blood oath their saint President Ronald Reagan of all thing good and angelic in economic growth and free markets miracles, which it only tepidly and occasionally materialized, but not in the series of recent jobless recoveries, when the fund went for wealth concentration among the very oligarchical few.

The fix in the fixed news is the attacks on legacy benefits, social security, pension, medical benefits have been coming from the megabanks, and ultra-wealthy takers, cooperate welfare queens, megacorporation and all of the other demagogic nonsense that comes out of mega-international-cooperation media spins.

The ethical high roads would have increased jobs, real income, governmental revenues, reparative solutions, immediately after the down turns.

Figure 8 shows nominal federal social benefit outlays.

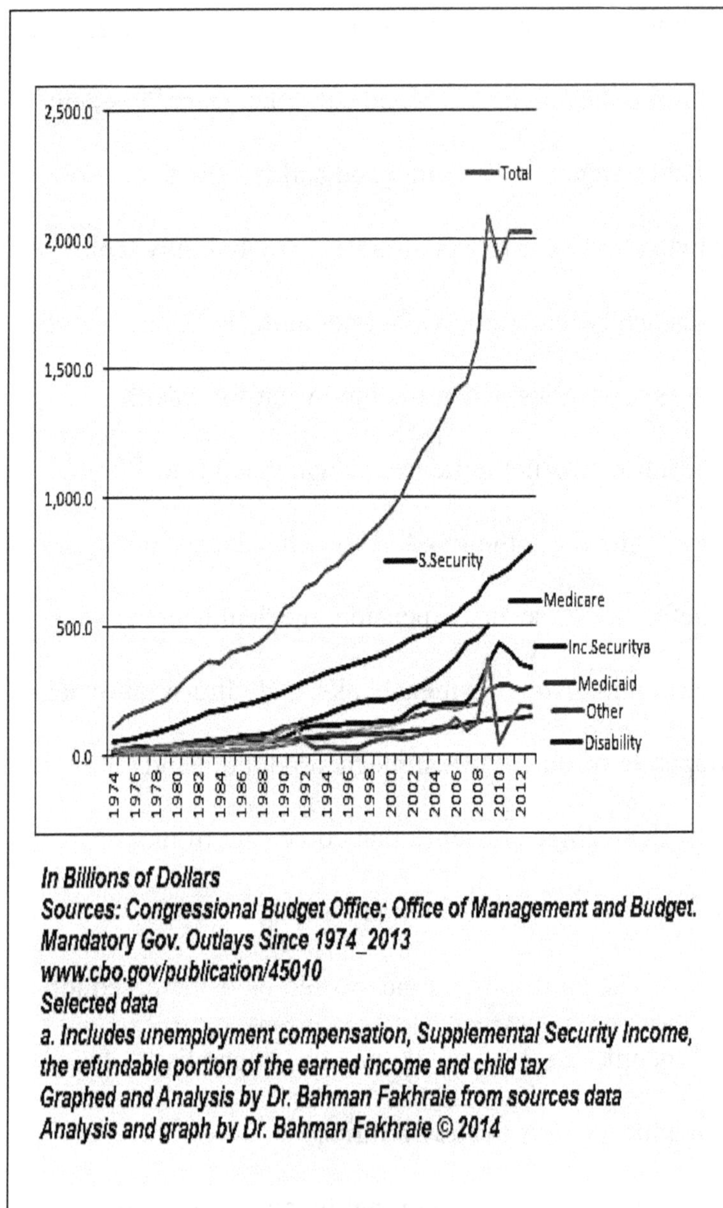
2,500.0
2,000.0
1,500.0
1,000.0
500.0
0.0
Total
S.Security
Medicare
Inc.Securitya
Medicaid
Other
Disability
1974
1976
1978
1980
1982
1984
1986
1988
1990
1992
1994
1996
1998
2000
2002
2004
2006
2008
2010
2012
In Billions of Dollars
Sources: Congressional Budget Office; Office of Management and Budget.
Mandatory Gov. Outlays Since 1974_2013
www.cbo.gov/publication/45010
Selected data
a. Includes unemployment compensation, Supplemental Security Income,
the refundable portion of the earned income and child tax
Graphed and Analysis by Dr. Bahman Fakhraie from sources data
Analysis and graph by Dr. Bahman Fakhraie © 2014

Figure 8, Federal social benefits outlays, 1974-2012.

Perhaps a lower CEO bonus path, a more modest rate of wealth accumulation for the mega-wealthy, would have eased the troughs, and repaired the down turn damages. Now, they will feel the fixes and the adjustments more. They are still screaming at the nation for cooperate comprehensive tax reduction for jobs, without the 30 percent cooperation minimum tax mandate. The middle class and working poor had deserved the tax breaks, the jobs, the wages, and RDI increases to raise the aggregate demand in the national economy. The GOP forgot their taxes were 80 percent when President Kennedy reduced them. Their taxes were 60 percent when President Reagan reduced them, again. Each time we had post-recession increase in employment and increase in RDI.

Figure 9 shows federal social benefit outlay as percentage of GDP. The increase in the curve shows the time of major economic downturn in USA economy.

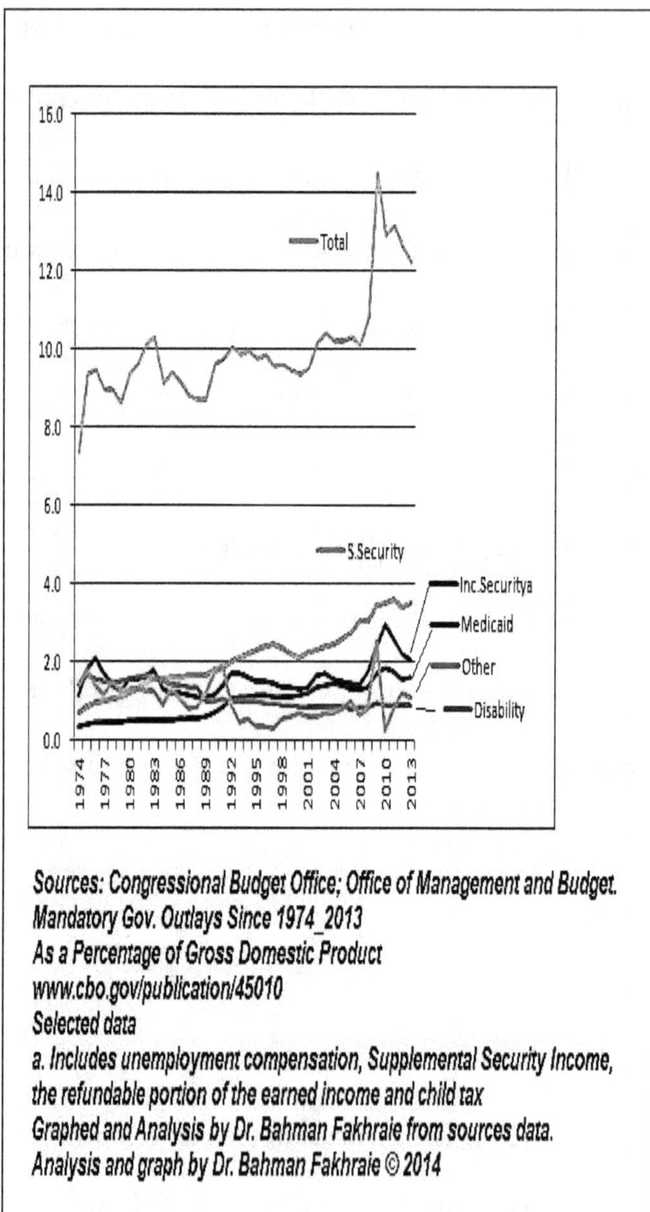

Figure 9, Federal social benefit outlay as percentage of GDP.

Those increased the government revenues from income increases at all level of incomes. It is also important to note, until before 2007, total federal social benefits stayed around 10 percent. Despite the permanent wars, and long GOP wars, and their damages to the economy, the social costs of mandatory outlays remained around 14 percent and declined. This is after, they caped the social security tax for people making over $100,000 a year salaries, without capping benefits. They also voted and removed the middle class brackets tax breaks. This is after the soldiers came home with multiple disabling issues. Moreover, the wealth concentration went to the few at the top, and RDI of middle class and working poor stayed flat, or declined.

Blaming the matter on the legacy benefits, low productivities, unions, workers-skill sets, under prepared graduates, and underfunded education systems are malicious purchased-spins to stop ethical contributions to job creations, and the future of this great nation. Clear sign adjustments have to be rectifying promptly. The check and balance have increase more prominently in operational functionalities of governmental, political, and economic organizations.

NOTE

[1] Ott, J. Steven, *The Organizational Culture Perspectives*, (Pacific Grove, California: Brooks/Cole Publishing Company, 1989).

[2] Bahman Fakhraie, PhD., *Political Monopolistic Capitalism, Wealth Concentration Schema : The Haves, The Have-Nothings, And The Have-Less*, Utah, FERDAT Publishing, 2014, https://www.createspace.com/4631870?ref=1147694&utm_id=6026

[3] Statistics of Income--Corporation Income Tax Returns (Publication 16). Additional data on the foreign tax credit and U.S. possessions tax credit from special in-depth studies are included in various issues of the Statistics of Income Bulletin.

[4] Data on corporate "Profits before tax (per NIPA)" are from the Bureau of Economic Analysis's National Income and Product Accounts, Table 1.12: National Income by Type of Income. This table appears in the Survey of Current Business and can be accessed online at: http://www.bea.gov/bea/dn/nipaweb/index.asp.
Data on "Net income (less deficit) (per SOI)" and "Income subject to tax (per SOI)" are from Statistics of Income—Corporation Income Tax Returns, various years.

[5] "Below are eight of the most clueless statements by the 1%, all of them made in the past 12 months."

Evan McMurry (Alternet), 8 stunning reminders of the 1 percent's unbelievable narcissism: Whether comparing justified public anger to the Holocaust or lynch mobs, America's mega-rich can't help themselves, SALON, Wednesday, Mar 5, 2014 06:43 AM -0700 http://www.salon.com/2014/03/05/8_stunning_reminders_of_the_1_percents_unbelievable_narcissism_partner/

[6] There are more press reports about cases that major cooperation have not paid taxes, and collected subsidies.

CHAPTER 3

MARKET IMPERFECTIONS

Imperfections in market competition are endogenous to self-inducements of the markets. The imperfections of perfect competitive assumptions will influence final costs, price, wage, rent, and interest depending on the market organizations of the modular production, and the organization of the buyer groups. These are classified under three general cases. That is, imperfections of competitive assumptions, oligopoly, duopoly, and monopoly versus monopsony. The effects on the markets are as follows.

$$Qc < Qd,o < Qm$$
$$Pm > Pd,o > Pc$$

The presence of any barriers to modular production process, like new technology or skill, or barrier to entry to the market place, or litigious blockages to production or entry initiates upward price alterations, and reduction in quantity presented to the markets.[1] The clear implications at the value theory microeconomic levels are that quantities supplied reduce, and price of differentiated or rare items increase.

One the most modern example of technological duopoly is MS-PC with MS operating system, and Apple-PC, which have had parallel development for differentiated products, but there are older technologies and mature products. They influenced higher than normal prices of PCs until recently, when prices went below $400 ranges.

They have reduced number of workers in each operational facility comparative to manufacturing facilities, and they have formulated policies. In some cases, they have kept their taxes lower for entrepreneurial purgative and enfant industry portion far too long. There are newer technological clusters that have challenged the uniqueness nature of computer industry duopoly.

The digitalization, mobile-technologies, and wireless internet connectivity, and larger number of modular producers in the newer nanotechnologies, therefore the technological industries have pushed quantity of products higher, and their prices of product-packages below $200. This trend will continue for sometimes.

The manufactured the financial market disasters of this millennium at one hand, and the garnished political forces behind the taxpayers bail out at the other hand, inquire what kind of governance allowed them to flourish unattended, and then mushroom globally.[2] All events require honest holistic teconomic analysis.

Plutocracy, Technocracy

The organizational drifts from the pull of competitive incentives to imperfect competitions enticements of wealth concentration of oligopoly and plutocracy, and further to monopolistic market forces and oligarchies have dominated the last few decades. The

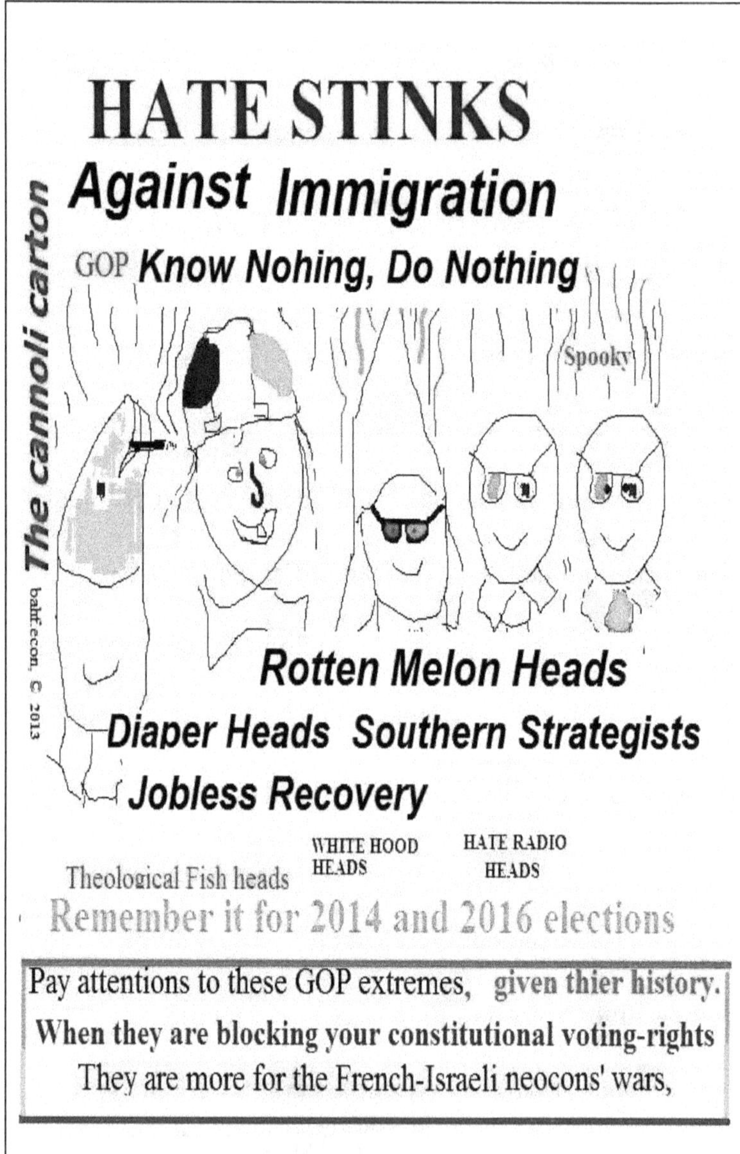
HATE STINKS
Against Immigration
GOP Know Nohing, Do Nothing
Spooky
The cannoli carton
bahf.econ, © 2013
Rotten Melon Heads
Diaper Heads Southern Strategists
Jobless Recovery
WHITE HOOD HEADS
HATE RADIO HEADS
Theological Fish heads
Remember it for 2014 and 2016 elections
Pay attentions to these GOP extremes, given thier history.
When they are blocking your constitutional voting-rights
They are more for the French-Israeli neocons' wars,

substantial social and private costs leveled at free enterprise economic systems taxpayers. Financial market crash, institutional bankruptcy, and governmental interventionism with jobless-recovery seem to be fading memories in wait for the reappearing of undiscovered-unrepentant sinners.

Yet, there are no limits to their greed agenda, and their attempts to victimize the unemployed, structurally unemployed graduates, the middle class, and working poor. Do you remember, when they said cooperation limitless money in election is free speech and it will not affect your financial conditions, or your economy? All the while, their GOP representatives, Democratic Party helpers, media enablers have arranged the tax codes differently.

They arranged the social costs to come out of diminishing lower tax brackets and income of individual-taxpayers, not cooperation minimum taxes.[3] These individuals have had flat or declining real incomes due to the nature of economic down turn.

Figure 10 shows millennial nominal private fixed investments in major economic sectors. The digital and software enfant industries show more sustained private fixed investment than the residential sector of the economy.

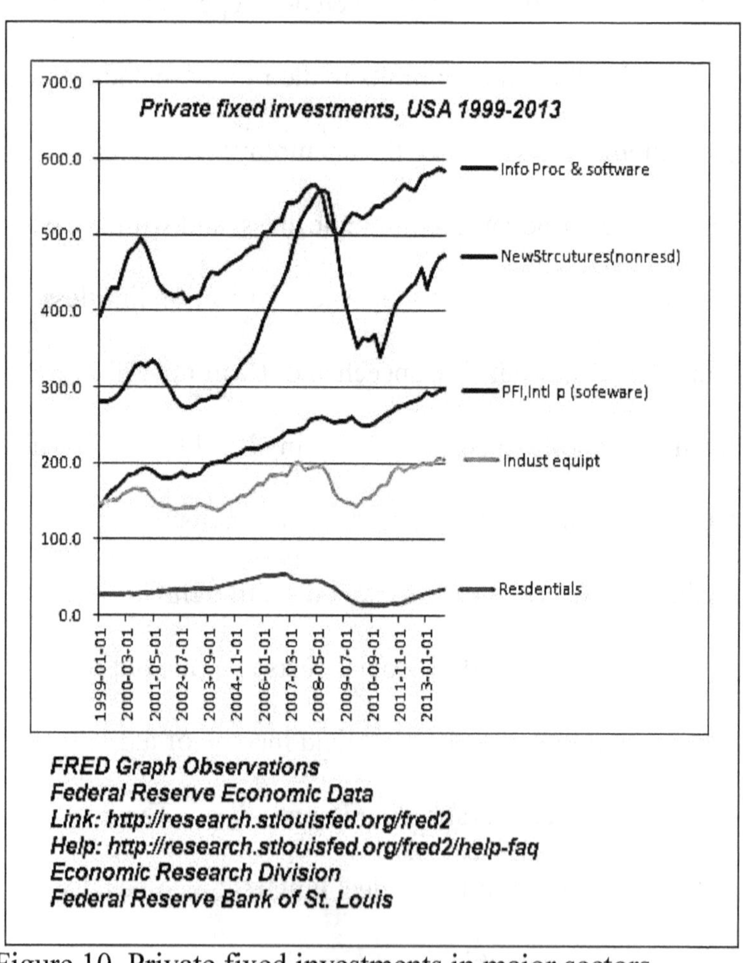

Figure 10, Private fixed investments in major sectors.

MINIMUM COOPERATE TAXATION

Those purchased laws and class warfare on majority of American citizens internally, by the uneducated ultra-wealthy, and their mega cooperate citizens have affected government revenue and your taxes, your benefits, and still have not made enough jobs. That is their plutocracy and technocracies, and oligarchies have failed, and these next three provisos prove their failures.

The trends for nominal private investments in all major sectors are positive after main recession cycles. The one exception in the graph is the residential structures, which has been flat. There are three provisos with these otherwise bright and supposedly illuminating pictures. One is residential structures, flat or declining nominal private investment in that sector is bad for overall jobs indices. Two is the nominal numbers increases have to be verified or falsified by the real increases in the indices for a scientific affirmation or hypothesis-rejection.

The third provisory condition has already proven difficult, too. That is the balancing comprehensive immigration fixes. After breaking the system, it will cost them even more. Even if they pulled a fast one to make taxpayers pay the megabank miss-investments.[4] It is getting harder to fool all of the people, even in the off year's elections.

Nevertheless, a scientific presentation can simplify the conundrums. Indeed, if real private investment have declined, despite the nominal increase, and real disposable income per population have declined, the cooperate tax revenues have dropped, the national economy will suffer. Because aggregate demand will dissipate, and logarithmic real growth rate of GDP will decline. Moreover, all cooperate manipulation will not remedy the events, expo facto. Hence, their plutocratic economic models have failed.

Their answer will be to cut the social security, and social safety nets, Medicare, legacy private contracts, increase full time hours, and cut government jobs and all. That will compound the problem form cyclical recessions into major economic down turn, jobless recoveries, and into 1933 type of a depression. Given, we are in none-functionality phase of our political cycles, the probabilities of the worst event occurrences due to fiscal policies none-functionality increases, regardless of monetary policies.

NOTE

[1] William Fellner, *Competition Among the Few: Oligopoly and Similar Market Structures*, New York, August M. Kelly Publisher, 1965

[2] Dr. Bahman Fakhraie, Teconomic Analysis of Cascading Millennial Economies, Utah, FERDAT Publishing, ISBN-97809852968, https://www.createspace.com/4187823

[3] Congressional Budget Office; Office of Management and Budget. Mandatory Gov. Outlays since 1974_2013 www.cbo.gov/publication/45010

[4] Bahman Fakhraie, PhD., TECONOMICS OF VERBALISM, Ogden, Utah, FERDAT publishing, 2013, https://www.createspace.com/4121720 ISBN-978-0-9852958-4-4,

CHAPTER 4

MARKET AND POLITICAL SYSTEMS

Market organizations and political systems have long interdependent coexistence that at times may go out of balance, if unchecked. These producers and CEOs, in technological oligopoly fields, and mega investment banks, and mega-internationals have garnished wealth concentration. The organizational development has advanced around self-serving pay structures, the unethical version of X-managements techniques, and wealth concentrations. Thus, an atmospheric change in governance, which have benefited from technological and governmental regulations forms of oligopoly and monopoly organizational controls and blocks have been garnished toward those tasks.

Therefore, they have utilized both market and political organizational-technologies to monetize their strategies around the X-managerial and operational systems. In the past when we studied mathematical multivariable optimization, Sheppard Lemma, the assumptions were that market forces acted alone, however, in Dr. Bahman Fakhraie's Sustainability Lemma new dimensions are studied that influence, complement or extend duration of market forces. The extensive utilization of political organization influences, and market influences have monetized and extended the duration of market activities. They have influenced wages, prices, and shareholders pay at (value theory for the firms' operational level). The removal of Glass Steagle act, modifications of cooperate tax rate, nullifications, burden-transference, transparency controls, and manipulations of tax rates of the upper tax brackets will constitute the vigorous existences of these adjunct-organizational powers. These economic organizations are targeting economic policies, instead of traditional, complementary, managerial efficiencies and functional fiscal policies. They are acting collectively in a harmful manner. They have been successful enough to induce funding. It will not be difficult to assume they will mushroom in form of political organizations to influence elections, votes, voting regulations, and policies in other directions than free democratic public votes, or free flow of public opinions. They will ultimately introduce malleability to democratic principles toward wealth concentration mechanism, than wealth creation sustainability of free market systems.

That will make them (plutocracy or oligarchy) extremisms in some cases. Therefore, they act counterproductive to the competitive free market economics principles. They have affected workers and national income at the aggregate data level, too.[1] Hence, they have reduced employment nationally by increasing unemployment rates and in reducing re-employment rates structurally.

The harming of domestic housing industry had a great impact on domestic economic growth, income inequalities, and jobs creations, in the millennium down turn. They did this at the supply side, by harming domestic mortgage industries, and at the demand side, by inflicting real disposable income depression, and promotion of jobless recoveries.

The computerization, digitization, and smart robotics have introduced structural adjustment in re-employment rates, in most cases with substantial tax-breaks and subsidies, which do not go to benefit the structurally unemployed, but they are offered to the new factories, or industrial arrangements with more knowledge-capital intensive-technologies at state and federal levels. Therefore, economic recovery will require specific monetary and fiscal remedies tailored for the events that are an essential aspect of economic recovery, which will encourage job creationism, temporarly.

SYMBIOTIC ORGANIZATIONAL Y-MATRIX

The cultural adjustments can replace the obsolete an outdated X-Techniques with a managerial Y-Matrix strategy, which will remain accommodative and foundational to modern technological paradigm.[2] Thus, the core values of tasks are accomplished with self-fulfillments, and satisfaction of invisible hands. Moreover, the matrix allows for multiple disciplinary participations, for more complex collective tasks, which will include profits, and optimizations. Therefore, the strategies for organizational development will accommodate planned changes flexible to internal and external factors.

The organizations will need to comply, and be accommodative to the recovery. Especial taxes on such organizational activities may be required to educate public of their rules and policy intends, and to comply with the transparency of democracy. The least active fiscal policy side, will need to raise taxes of the cooperate entities at the top one percent highest brackets from 10 percent or lower (zero, or negative rates) to 30 percent minimum cooperate tax rate (MCTR).

A portion of that government revenue will have to go to retaining and job-creation, if we adopt the Y-Matrix managerial teconomic strategies advanced here. The job-creation involves state and federal infrastructural replacement projects, with retraining for secondary positions, placements, or vertical job placements. The cooperation and free enterprise employment with living wages will increase in such recoveries as they arrive cyclically.

A good portion of that government-revenue have to be transferred to an standalone earned income tax credit (EITC) for middle class and lower income earners, especially in jobless recovery counter cycle epochs. Even, if we still insist to follow the supply sides' obsolete model of X-managerial (CEOs-self-promotion) arrangements.

MULTICULTURALISM AND LEGAL IMMIGRANTS

Political discrimination, anti-multiculturalism, and anti-legal immigrants' laws are visceral emotionalism ascribed, thus they are not helpful to the progress of an economic recovery, and the longevity of this constitutional experiment in democratic republic.

They have garnished organizational supports from neo-Nazis, skinheads, Southern Strategist, xenophobes, and anti-multicultural international terrorist gangs. Those negative political organizations have influenced harmful laws to American economic, and they are influencing lawmakers to detriment of better economic optimality conditions and economic jobless recoveries.

The implications of these two major impacts of organizational forces on economic optimizations and recovery efforts are their negative counter cyclical natures. That will make them important to economic policy and national economic wellbeing in a difficult economic time.

One can opine constitutionally that the reason ultra-wealthy Americans are concerned about policy so much, it is because they paid for so much of it to be ignored. Perhaps, they do not want to be treated, as the immigrants and legal immigrant-Americans, by the hate-agenda they (some of them) have financed so much. For one, I do not blame or dismiss their concerns; however, they paid and are paying for these anti-immigrants' monstrosity laws among other bad laws. Why would terrorizing 14th amendment American children and youth get a pass from xenophobes and new laws? Americans have to check these negative organizational tendencies for their own economic self-interests, beside the constructive positive ethics, or the ignored morality sakes.

Laws to monetize or criminalize immigrants' productivities, and legal immigrants daily lives are pushed in many states and DC. Laws that tear up families, and familial links and financial lives, are not unlike the Federal

Reserve policies that extended duration of the 1930 depression. They have to be filtered and checked regularly.

The millennial cyclical economic activities have had down turns in the employment numbers, too. Nevertheless, the upturns have not had increase in the employment typical of their history.

In the book (Teconomics*), the complex population-age components were discussed more substantially.[3] The complexity and components of millennial private investments have also been detailed. Therefore, it is more alarming that updating our fiscal policy formulations devolved into ideological mud fields, into dangerous extremes and none-functionality.

Indeed, did external-terrorism inflict so much harm, to derail the national economic resolve to advance welfare and income of all workers and citizens? Did someone there spend our national accumulated wealth, deteriorating our advanced educated systems, and stopping fiscal policy responses exogenously? Taxpayers spent 17 trillion dollars over a decade. That is divide among the 7 billion estimate of global population is $2,428 per soul globally. Still, it takes a few pennies a day to feed most hungry masses. Alas, we have hungry population globally. Are we spending our resources wisely?

Internally, a system reboot will require readjustments of some ethical mishandlings, in politics, business, finance, mega-wealthy lobbyism, their cash in politics, and economics organizations.

Figure 11 does not show a validation of the hypothesis that unemployment rate fluctuations and cyclical upturns are substantial and normal.[4] Therefore, the hypothesis is rejected.

The Popperian falsification of the same hypothesis is shown in the civilian labor-force-participation rate. It has been declining since 1999. The rejection of hypothesis is reconfirmed in the decrease in the employments per population rate, which has paralleled the decline in the unemployment rates in the same graph.

The proposition was presented that structural unemployment has been confirmed among the working population 25 year and older. That will require intervention by public initially, but by both public and private organizational market forces.

The explanation for the multiple confirmation of structural unemployment are three folds, one is the retirement of baby boomers. Two is the implosions of legal immigration regulations since 1996 act, and organization obsceneness to reparatory fixes. Three, is the decline of real minimum wage, and its substantial diversion from the living wage.

Figure 11 shows labor participation and unemployment per capita rates, of college graduate over age 25, employment per population, and civilian unemployment rate.

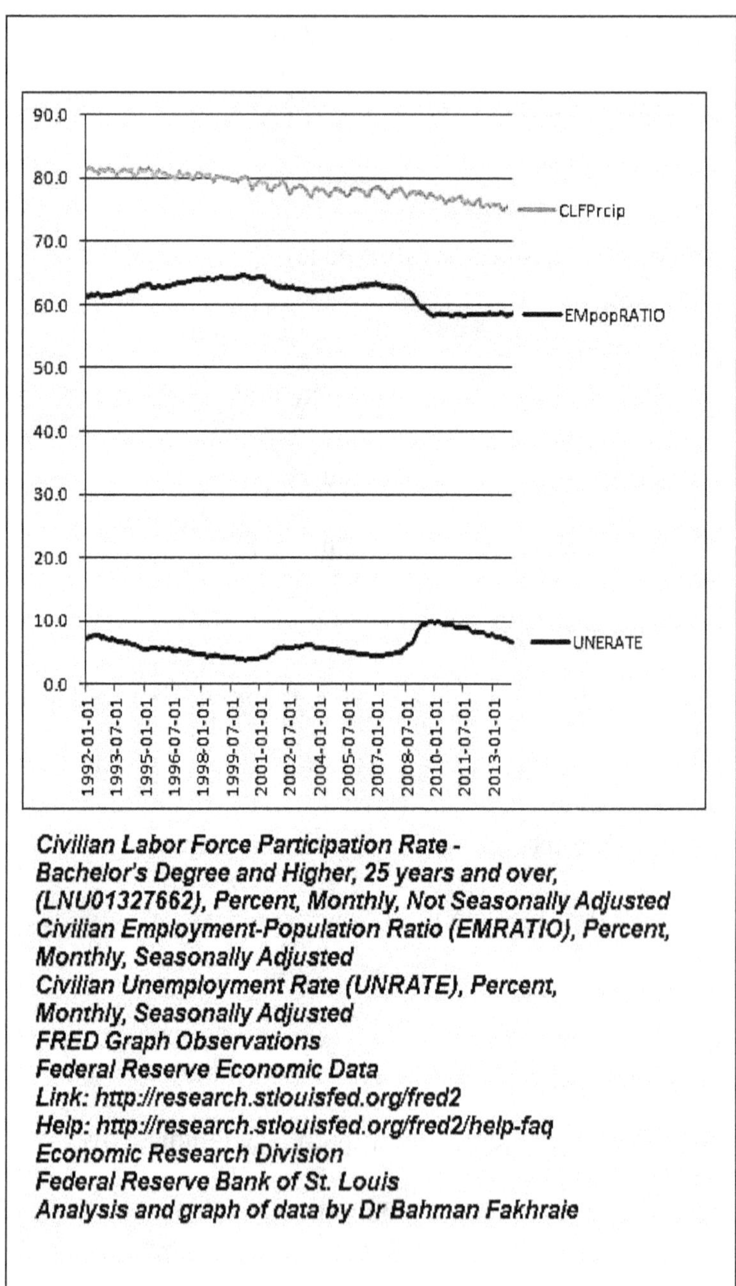
90.0
80.0
70.0
60.0
50.0
40.0
30.0
20.0
10.0
0.0
CLFPrcip
EMpopRATIO
UNERATE
1992-01-01
1993-07-01
1995-01-01
1996-07-01
1998-01-01
1999-07-01
2001-01-01
2002-07-01
2004-01-01
2005-07-01
2007-01-01
2008-07-01
2010-01-01
2011-07-01
2013-01-01
Civilian Labor Force Participation Rate -
Bachelor's Degree and Higher, 25 years and over,
(LNU01327662), Percent, Monthly, Not Seasonally Adjusted
Civilian Employment-Population Ratio (EMRATIO), Percent,
Monthly, Seasonally Adjusted
Civilian Unemployment Rate (UNRATE), Percent,
Monthly, Seasonally Adjusted
FRED Graph Observations
Federal Reserve Economic Data
Link: http://research.stlouisfed.org/fred2
Help: http://research.stlouisfed.org/fred2/help-faq
Economic Research Division
Federal Reserve Bank of St. Louis
Analysis and graph of data by Dr Bahman Fakhraie

Figure 11, Civilian labor-force participation-rates.

Laws tax immigrant families of their pennies and dims, while their children, American children are in stress of law violations in going to colleges, and face the student loan heavy burdens, and graduate joblessness and inadequate wages. Laws that violate the 1st, 4th, 14th amendments of the United State constitution regularly, and other amendments frequently, laws that separate families forcibly, laws to e-verify and segregate, and miss treat large segment of the society anti-constitutionally, without probable cause, or legal foundations. The "Nazis-Kristallnacht" ultra-wealthy people know best, they can become these laws, or these organizations new victims. They will be called names, like ultra-wealthy RINOs on new petitions, too. Their wealth can be targeted readily. Government can countermand their private-contracts.

Quick laws can resent their social contracts with America, too. While constructional economic mobility could have remedied most of the class warfare divisive post-recession ailments. The fixed immigration laws could have increased government revenues, jobs, economic conditions, and velocity of money in increased circulation, and aggregate-demand, nationally and internationally, too.

POLITE, FUNCTIONAL, AND HUMANE POLITICS

There are no close comparative equivalences. The GOP machinery is already turning hate on immigrants, women, minority, elderly middle class, and poor Americans, for their 2014 campaign-agendas.

They have utilized the newness of citizens-united-cooperation laws into new negative political organizations, knowing the legal diversions of free speech and hate speech. They are doing it knowing the bad results, which are turning the 80 to 90 percent of all groups against them. Americans do not vote for hate group into office, they vote to get them out of their political offices.

Turning anti-science has consequences. Ask the politicians in those states that were not proactive to winter snow, before and after the last perfectly unhappy January 2014 snow and ice storm, and the last few tsunamis. Did their spin save them? The weather-persons-scientific defense will hurt their politics even more, in places they have not yet conjured.

Therefore, voters please tell them again to stay human, real, and functional Americans (as much as possible) on all issues and immigration-issues, because 2014 and 2016 are here and now.

Moreover, Americans usually do not vote for hate groups, or their chicken hawks into office. Just do not let them slow your logic down, by blocking your voting, they will charge you more for a voter-ID, you will use for few votes rarely. You stay in voting-queues more than others in their voting-districts do. Hoping you will go home. Vote your votes anyway. Make a special day to vote, and vote them out of office, if they are betraying the constitutional laws, find others who follow the constitution.

FOREIGN POLICY, SUPERIORITY PSYCHOSIS

The gestalt of our foreign policy toward Islamic nations, in Asia and Africa cannot be a Hopson choice between psychosis and schadenfreude. It has to be based on foundational of diplomacy and truth telling, potentially contradictory matters.

Otherwise, extremists, abstractionists, war profiteers, destructionists, international monopolists will drive our policy off and away from the progressive roads that help sustain our economy most.

The people of these nations like our middle classes have to see a positive drive and an agenda of peace and prosperity, a constructionists' plan ahead for themselves and their children.

American voters cannot be mollified for long, by xenophobic, racists, sexist, and hate-speech derangements syndromes (HDS, and other psychosis ailments), which have afflicted the right wing-nuts, and the hate radio and multimedia dim-lights. The voters do not vote hate.

It is all too much, too much to ask a broken political party not to morph into another hate-group, while it is fading away from polite politics, and joining the free market purchased monetization of politics, and lobbyists industrial complexes, and negative organizations. The anti-immigrant degeneration of modern politics, the anti-science fervor, these are all accumulative and destructive negative economic externalities.

The technological enhancements of such skill sets have hastened devolutionary forces, which will leave an indelible mark on exceptionalness of any philosophically advanced and thinking culture. It has ended many powerful hate groups of history. At 100 to 400 million-dollar tickets, purchased democracies, politicians, and laws are no longer representative democratic republics, but agenda organizations, and some hate and negative-agenda organizations. Unless there are traces of truthful dictum (of the people, by the people, and for the people) in the vestige-nature of such organization, it will be hard to see them as patriotic tools.

American people like people around the globe, they do not give up on themselves, when they discover the differences between the hidden fingers, instead of the invisible relative free market hands, the costs are too dear to us all and to the democratic republics.

Otherwise, how will a society countermand the impacts of accumulative inequalities and powerful destabilizing forces unlocked by profiteering of imperfect-competition economics, and political monopolistic capitalism accumulatively? The logic is not there.

The Nazis (no disrespect intended to great and kind German people) among others were never convinced, of the imperfections of their implosive economic philosophy or the inevitabilities of global complications after their savage colonial dirt-wars. Yet, like other cultures north and south, east and west, the scholar did learn fanatical delusions make harmful companions for time travelers of history.

Some assumed mistakenly, that technologies would compensate for foundational terminal logics, fiscal policy nonexistence, deliberate financial crimes, organizational mischief-makers, and governmental nihilistic paralysis. It has been a mistake, to ignore corrective constructional relatively-perfectly competitive-free-market signals, which do fall short ominously faster outside democratic functionalities.

Therefore, polite, functional, constructional, bipartisan, diplomatic, domestically intensive economic policies and humane politics are good models that pay positive dividends for the holistic teconomics models of the future, in time.

American people and democratic nations generally have corrective instincts, which are capable of correcting mistaken side trips, for shared economic growth and developmental steps. Therefore, in the light of better paradigms, the future looks optimistically bright, considering all other alternatives.

NOTE

[1] William Fellner, Competition Among the Few: Oligopoly and Similar Market Structures, New York, August M. Kelly Publisher, 1965

[2] Bahman Fakhraie, PhD., TECONOMICS, Utah, FERDAT Publishing, 2010
ISBN/EAN13: 0985295813 / 9780985295813,
https://www.createspace.com/4196760
Alan Bullock, and Oliver Stallybrass, *The Harper Dictionary Of Modern Thought,* New York, Harper and Row, 1977

[3] Ibid,2010

[4] Congressional Budget Office; Office of Management and Budget. Mandatory Gov. Outlays since 1974_2013
www.cbo.gov/publication/45010

CHAPTER 5

SUMMERY AND CONCLUSIONS

Certain economic systems accommodate economic recoveries better than others do. The free enterprise capitalist economies in general are assumed more accommodative to this notion. However, in this book there are documented reasons, why these systems have not performed well in this last recovery cycle.

SUMMERY

In summary condition for test of the hypothesis about nominal and real investments, for verification and falsifications were enumerated. The result is double-checked by the natural logarithmic measurement of growth rate of certain indices. Figures 10, the nominal private investments in major industries were discussed. It was noted that nominal graphs were looking positive in number of areas. The industries showing promises were information-processing software, new nonresidential structures, industrial equipment all favored an upward trend line, all but housing industries (residential).

Figure 12 shows the real private fixed investment, USA 1999-2013.

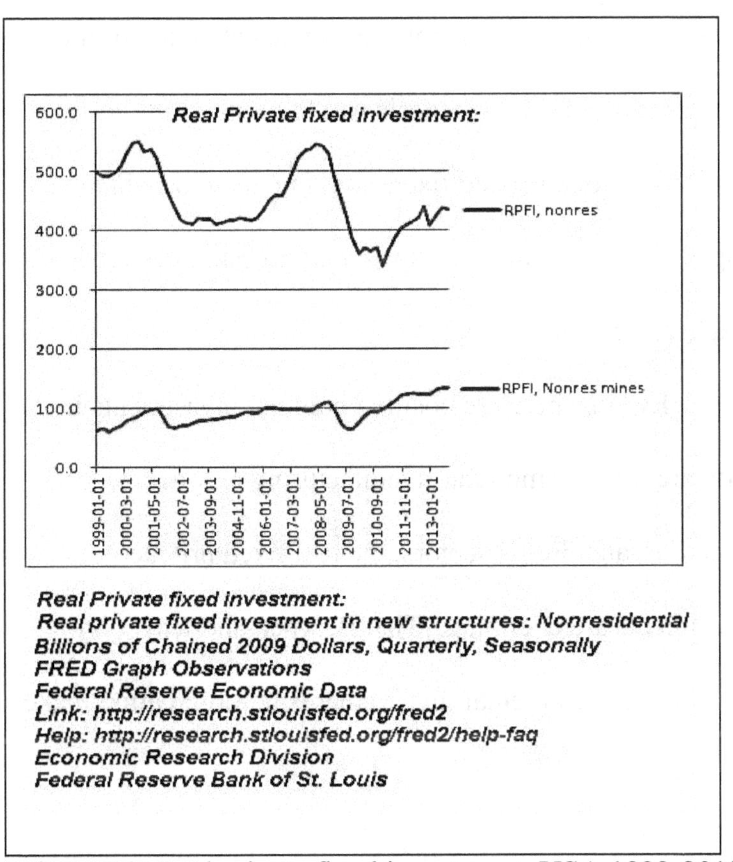

Figure 12, Real private fixed investment, USA 1999-2013.

That has declining trend line, and investment in mines that is flat or increased slightly. This graph is important in the Popperian test we established in this study.

The test of this hypothesis was to check the real privet investment for a more detailed trend line over time, which either confirmed and verified the positive trends, or falsified and reject the hypothesis, by negative trend line. The rejection of the hypothesis would require long-term trend-line of real private fixed investments to be negatively sloped. It will mean a decline in real investment overtime at aggregate economic level.

Even if there are positive nominal investments in software, robotic modular manufacturing production processes, and digital sectors, the real fixed private investments are declining. That is, when and why aggregate governmental involvements in job-creation make a difference.

The constructive population age mix of workers and taxpayers have been harmed by bad anti-family and xenophobic immigration policies, too. Unfortunately, even after reading the research, they are hoping some STEM-policy will pay off in 8-11 future years. Just how many more deep recessions they want the American economy to experience, knowing it will not affect their income brackets, or job status. How long, how many years is it rational for the structurally unemployed to pull themselves up by their own bootstraps?

Science tells us; hopefully, the opposition supply-siders are evolving too, whether they believe in it or not. Polite, Functional, and Humane Politics mean do not self-destruct your political party or national economic models for your private greed. Aggregate data trend-lines for rRDI (Growth Rate of Real Disposable Income), rRDIPC, and population growth rates stay flat or decline. Figure 13 shows growth rate for RDPI, RDPIPC, and population.

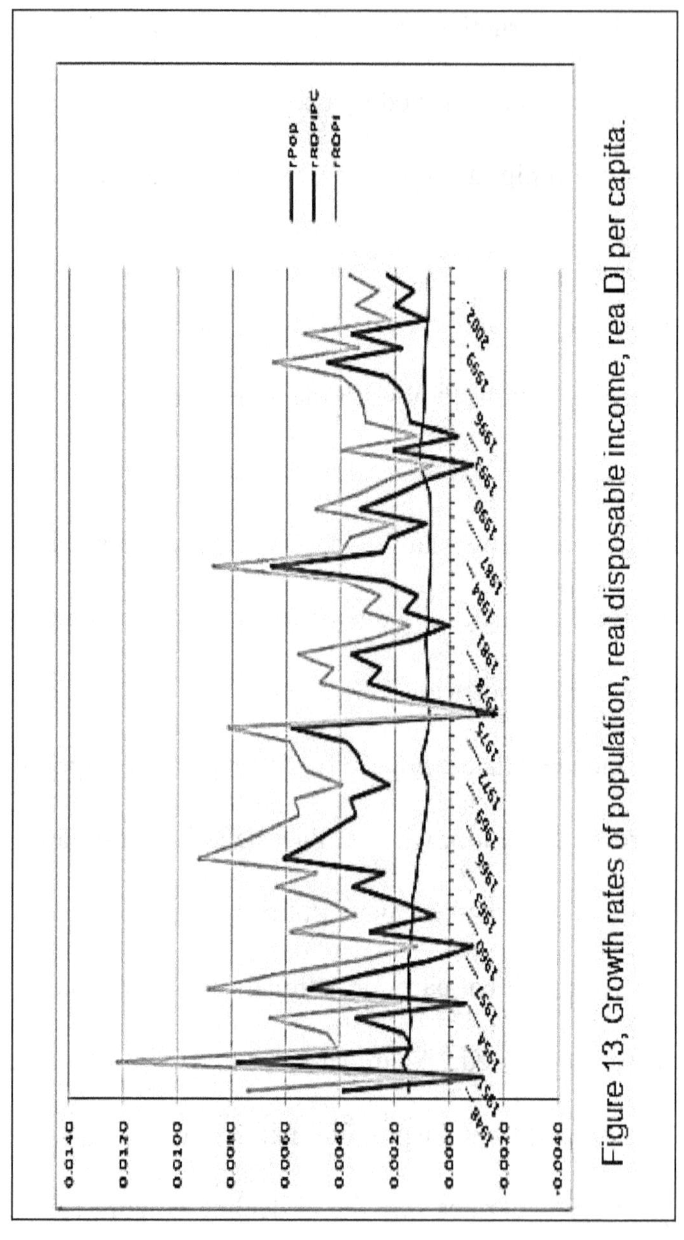

Figure 13, Growth rates of population, real disposable income, rea DI per capita.

While the wealth concentration of the top 1 percent or 0.01 percent occurs, in a Jobless-recovery cycle over time, distribution index illusion (DII) is formed. The mathematics and the books may have been too complicated. Here is a more accessible example in prose. In using aggregate data, rRDI, rRDIPC (Growth Rates of Real Disposable Personal Incomes per capita) indices have been used in my books for certain logical necessities. Because when Nash-disequilibrium game theory is used in policy, system tolerance allows sustainability to hold up to a threshold limit. There are specific preconditions that allow for systems tolerances. However, sustained reduction in aggregate demand will have consequences for joblessness.

Table 2 show a decision matrix formulated to study patterns of income distribution in a dynamically functional economy, and the risks associated with a few case studies of income distributions, expo facto.

Table 2, Distributions plus risks matrix.

Sustainability, Distributions, and risk-decisions Matrix (SDRM)				
Pop%, income brackets / Cases	50P/L	40P/M	10P/H	Total 100 %
A - ur	30/0.06	25/0.625	45/4.5	100 %
B +	35/0.7	45/1.1	20/2	100 %
C - prv	10/0.2	10/0.25	80/8	100 %
D -- prv	80/1.6	10/0.25	10/1.6	100 %

In this hypothetical example, there are 4 cases (A, B, C, D,). Potential for social unrest (ur), and pre-revolution thresholds (prv) are so designated. Fifty percent of population is low-income brackets, 40 percent is medium, and 10 percent are high-income brackets. Percent of national income going to each of three brackets groups and fractions going to per capital individual in the group designate are in inside cells. While cases C and D represent extremes, they are only approximate estimations and distributional estimations.

This is not a preset income distribution by governments, utopians Socialism, or Marxism Valhalla, but a warning and risks of social unrest matrix, which should alert the governments or the society to know, they have chosen unwisely and they will need to reassess their employment arrangements, rather than confiscatory redistributions.

Demagogues can scream, from a hysterical perspective, two extremes come to mind, French and Russian revolutions.

In modern time, the private contractors, job-creators may have to be supplemented or be induced to rectify their ways back on the more competitive relatively free market path. Fuller employments with living wages are part of that temporary fiscal arrangement.

CONCLUSION

Therefore, it is important that cooperate taxes reflect cooperate and business ethical contributions to the societal good.

They cannot take taxpayers incomes at time of distress, which they mostly caused, and after their crisis, the cooperate (citizens) entities revoked their own social contracts unilaterally, ex post.

Figure 14 shows average federal tax for total, individual, and cooperate rates at top 1 percent, 1979-2010.

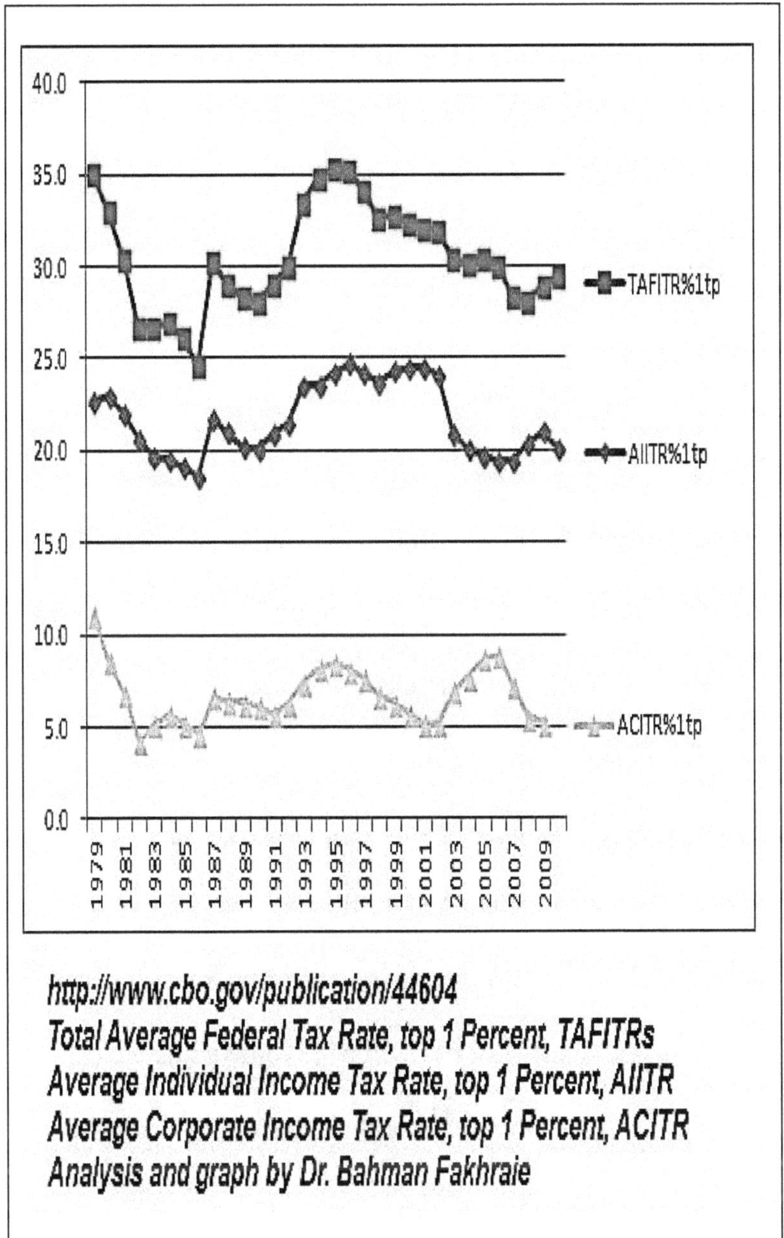

Figure 14, Average Federal Tax for total, individuals, and cooperate rates.

Especially, at the top one percent level, there should be cooperate-minimum-tax rates that maintain fiscal policy sustainability, somewhat at the level of average federal tax rates of top one percent individual-taxpayers. So, the uneducated mega-wealthy will not feel so victimized by their paid-cruel system!

There will be a definite revisiting of tax rates for the upper brackets, for tax and job-creation in full force. Perhaps another look at the USA-CBO tax rates will refresh your memories.[1] The tax rates for top one percent cooperation are the lowest for one reason and one reason only. When they cannot deliver that task, and fulfill the wealth creation by job-creations, when they turn risk-averse do not invest, their tax rates will need to be adjusted quickly, or indexed to increase the governmental revenue that will generate jobs for the recovering economics.

They will need to pay the same amount as the individuals, the teachers, the firepersons, police officers, professors, and the working secretaries, or the lucky few at the top one percent tax and income brackets levels, so government can finish their tasks and to ensure a sufficient aggregate demand. The minimum 30 percent flat tax sound just perfect for cooperation over two million dollar gross incomes.

The federal government (fiscal economic policy) must make sure that the increased government revenues goes to job-creation and not crony-capitalism, reelection crocodile-funds at state or federal levels, or any other purposes, or return it to small businesses that do create most of jobs, even with the mandatory level of living wages.

However ignoring a wrong path will cause more problems. One can read 1920s-1930s United Sates economic history, or more recent structural unemployment shortcomings and wealth concentration. The economic wisdom fall short of mark, when imperfect competition, monopolies, oligopolies tweak the economy into the wealth concentration path, by greed or criminal crony capitalism. Adam smith invisible hand or economic sciences have nothing to do with the oligopoly and monopoly greed shuffles and the cooperation-tax-dodging.

Therefore, in that logical light, wealth concentration, and negative private fixed investment, and collusions among monopolistic and other imperfect comparative organization forces in aggregate economy are rearrangements that add to deteriorations of sustainability conditions enough to imply system reactions, negative or positive. The mindset of "what is mine is mine, and what the rest of societies produce, are mine too," are conflict-intensive mindsets, it is not diplomatic, or cooperative, nor is it a constructively productive policy. It is true that after tax revenue and private contracts must hold firmly and honestly in a free market, for it to exist.

Even mildly restated, the accumulation of negative forces gathers momentums, under certain conditions. Human history of conflicts and social discontents should be enough to pick our interest.

It is important for the top one percent to internalize that the economy is a shared free market, or relatively free market economic system, especially if they are paying the most taxes for its continuums, to rephrase Churchill, it is the best system given the relative conditions of all other economic systems. Purchase and replacement of these systems by different political economic systems will have definite unproductive results, contrary to their best welfare and interests of all classes.[2] The top class will always have the most benefit in protecting the sustainability of just, employed, and productive economy.

Optimistically, in order to change the vector of a falling star, the further away from the event (earth) you start the better is chances for successful result. That is the star bypassing the earth instead of a collision with it. In social condition and societal order, the sooner we know of gathering problems, with the loud presumptions of functionality, the wiser and less costly will be our remedy-decisions.

It is optimistically a better wiser economic path, than the none-functionality path of devolution. Since the engine of economic advancement have gathered some steams, it is important to make sure ethical lapses do not harm the economic advancements, and all goes well with both the supply and demand sides gradual stepping upwards, optimistically.

NOTES

[1] Average Federal Tax Rates for All Households, by Before-Tax Income Group, 1979 to 2010 (Percent). http://www.cbo.gov/publication/44604

[2] Bahman Fakhraie, PhD., *Analytical Remedies for The Millennial Cascading Economic Declines*, Utah FERDAT Publishing 2012,
https://www.createspace.com/4187823,
Books web page at, http://bahfecon.wix.com/bahfecon,
Author books, http://www.amazon.com/Dr.-Bahman-Fakhraie/e/B00IKAR1CM/ref=ntt_athr_dp_pel_1

SELECTED BIBLIOGRAPHY

Bailey, Martin J., *National Income and the Price Level: A Study in Macroeconomic Theory,* New York: McGraw-Hill, 1971.

Baumol, William J., *Economic Theory and Operational Analysis,* 4th ed., New Jersey: Prentice-Hall, 1977.

Blaug, Mark, *Economic Theory in Retrospect,* 3rd Ed., London: The Cambridge University Press, 1978.

Böhn_Bawerk, Eugen Von., *Capital and Interest: Positive Theory of Capital,* vol. II, Trans. G. D. Hunt & H. F. Sennholz, Chicago: Libertarian Press, 1959.

Boulding, Kenneth E., *Economics As A science*, New York: McGraw-Hill Book Company, 1970.

Byers, Lloyd L., *Concept of Strategic Management: Planning and Implementation*, New York: Harper & Row Publishers.

Caves, Richard E. and Jones, R. W., *World Trade and Payments: An Introduction*, 2nd ed., Boston: Little, Brown and Company, 1977.

Chiang, Alpha C., *Fundamental Methods of Mathematical Economics*, 2nd ed., New York: McGraw-Hill Book Company, 1974.

Coombs, Philip H., *The World Educational Crisis: A System Analysis*, London: Oxford University Press, 1968.

Domar, Evsey D., *Essays in the Theory of Economic Growth*, New York: Oxford University Press, 1957, 154-167, 168, 181.

Druker, Peter F., *Innovation and Entrepreneurship*, New York: Harper & Row Publishers, 1985.

Eisner, R. "Depreciation Allowances, Replacement Requirement, and Growth," *The American Economic Review*, XLII, December 1952.

Dr. Bahman Fakhraie, *Teconomic of Verbalism,* Utah, FERDAT publishing 2012, and
Paperback link is at, https://www.createspace.com/4121720
The EBook Link is at,
http://www.amazon.com/dp/B00B1LO7UQ
Books web page at, http://bahfecon.wix.com/bahfecon

—. The Demand and Supply Sides of Appropriate Technological Advancement. (Research paper at University of Utah Economics Dept. 2003),

—. *Teconomics: the microeconomic analysis*, Utah, FERDAT publishing 2012, and,
https://www.createspace.com/4196760, Books web page at,
http://bahfecon.wix.com/bahfecon

—. *Demand and supply Sides of Technological Injections*, Utah, FERDAT Publishing, 2004, And at,
http://www.amazon.com/dp/098529583X/ref=rdr_ext_tmb
#reader_098529583X

—. *Technological injection, dynamic new capital measurements, and Production Theory in Economics*, (Michigan: ProQuest LLC, 2010) and, https://order.proquest.com/OA_HTML/pqdtibeCCtpItmDspRte.jsp
Books web page at, http://bahfecon.wix.com/bahfecon

—. *Teconomics of Verbalism*, Utah FERDAT Publishing 2012, and at, https://www.createspace.com/4121720,
Books web page at, http://bahfecon.wix.com/bahfecon

—. *Analytical Remedies for The Millennial Cascading Economic Declines,* Utah FERDAT Publishing 2012, and at, https://www.createspace.com/4187823,
Books web page at, http://bahfecon.wix.com/bahfecon,
Author books, http://www.amazon.com/Dr.-Bahman-Fakhraie/e/B00IKAR1CM/ref=ntt_athr_dp_pel_1

—. *Teconomics of Dynamic Risks: All Natural Disasters, And Energy resource Production Disasters*, Utah FERDAT Publishing 2013,
, http://www.amazon.com/Teconomics-Dynamic-Risks-Disasters-Resource/dp/0985295856/ref=la_B00IKAR1CM_1_4/175-7073716-3994312?s=books&ie=UTF8&qid=1394043193&sr=1-4

—. *Teconomics of Dynamic Sustainable Budgets,* Utah FERDAT Publishing 2013,
http://www.amazon.com/Teconomics-Dynamic-Sustainable-Budgets-Teconomic/dp/098945391X/ref=la_B00IKAR1CM_1_5/175-7073716-3994312?s=books&ie=UTF8&qid=1394043193&sr=1-5#reader_098945391X
Books web page at, http://bahfecon.wix.com/bahfecon,
Author books, http://www.amazon.com/Dr.-Bahman-Fakhraie/e/B00IKAR1CM/ref=ntt_athr_dp_pel_1

—. *POLITICAL MONOPOLISTIC CAPITALISM, WEALTH CONCENTRATION SCHEMA, UNITED*

STATES TECONOMIC ANALYSIS, 2014, Utah FERDAT Publishing 2014, http://www.amazon.com/Political-Monopolistic-Capitalism-Wealth-Concentration/dp/0989453995/ref=la_B00IKAR1CM_1_3_title_0_main/175-7073716-3994312?s=books&ie=UTF8&qid=1394043193&sr=1-3#reader_0989453995

—. "Economic Theories and Practices in Technological Changes, capital measures, and Production." (Research paper at University of Utah Economics Dept. 1988)

—. "Hallowing headless nations: the need to invest on public education under the 1980s international economic conditions," (Research paper at University of Utah Economics Dept. 1988)

—. "Transfer of Technologies and Socioeconomic Theories of Dualism," (Research paper at University of Utah Economics Dept. 1983)

Friedman, Milton and Schwartz, Anna Jacobson, *The Great Contraction 1929-1933*, vol.2, 2nd ed., New Jersey: Princeton University Press, 1973

Gander, James Patrick., *Technological Change and Raw Materials*, Salt Lake City: Bureau of Economic and Business Research, University of Utah, 1977.

Gardner, Ackley., *Macroeconomics: Theory and Policy*, New York: Macmillan Publishing Co., 1978.

Girton, Lance and Roper Don, "Theory and Implication of Currency Substitution," *Journal of Money, Credit, and Banking,* 13, no. 1 (February 1981): 12-30.

Hayek, Friedrich August Von., "Kapitalaufzehrung." Weltwirtschaftliches Archive 36, 1932, II, 86-108.

Heilbroner, Robert L., *The Worldly Philosophers*, New York: Time Inc., Special Ed., 1962.

Hicks, Sir John, *The Crisis in Keynesian Economics*, New York: Basic Books, Inc. 1974.

Hirshleifer, Jack, *Investment, Interest, and Capital*, New Jersey: Prentice-Hall, 1970.

—. *Time, Uncertainty, and Information*, New York: Basil Blackwell, 1989.

—. *Price Theory and Applications*, New Jersey: Prentice-Hall, 1976.

Henderson, J. M. and Quandt, R. E., *Microeconomic Theory; A Mathematical Approach*, 2nd ed., New York: McGraw-Hill, 1972. 191-199, 280

Hunt, E. K. and Howard J. Sherman, Economics*: An Introduction to Traditional and Radical Views*, 2nd Ed., San Francisco: Harper and Row Publishers, 1975.

Intriligator, Michael D., *Econometric Models, Techniques, and Applications*, New Jersey: Prentice-Hall, 1978.

Johnson, J., *Econometric Methods*. New York: McGraw-Hill, 1972.

Kant, Immanuel, *Critique of Judgment*, Trans. J. H. Bernard, New York: Hafner, 1951.

Kennedy Charles and Thirlwall, A.P., "Surveys in Applied Economics: Technological Progress," *The Economic Journal*, March 1972: 12.

Keynes, John Maynard, *Essays in Biography*, London: The Cambridge University Printing House for Royal Economic Society, 1972.

—. *The General Theory of Employment, Interest and Money,* 1st ed. 1936, London: The Cambridge University Printing House for Royal Economic Society, Reprint 1973.

Kindleberger, Charles P., *The World in Depression 1929-1939*, Los Angeles: University of California Press, 1973.

Kirzner, I.M., *Discovery and the Capitalist Process*, Chicago: University of Chicago Press, 1985.

Klein, P. A. and Moore, G. H., *Monitoring Growth Cycles in Market-Oriented Countries*, (Mass.: published for N. B. E. R., by Ballinger publishing Co., 1985).

Knight, Farnk H., *Risk, Uncertainty and Profit*, Chicago: University of Chicago Press, 1985.

Landes, David S., *The wealth and poverty of nations: Why Some are So Rich and Some are So Poor*, (New York: W.W. Norton & Company, 1998).

Lindert, Peter H. and Kindleberger Charles P., *International Economics,* 7th Ed., Illinois: Richard Irwin, 1982.

Mansfield, Edwin, *Technological Change*, New York: W. W. Norton & Co., 1971.

Mark, Blaug, *Economic Theory in Retrospect*, 3rd Ed. London: The Cambridge University Press, 1978.

Marx, K. (In a letter he wrote to Engel, dated 20 August, 1862, London), (handout by Professor Randa, 2004)

McKinnon, Ronald I., *Money and Capital in Economic Development*, Washington D. C.: The Brookings Institution, 1973.

Mensch, Gerhard, Das *technilogische Patt*., Frankfurt: Umschau Verlag, 1975.

—, *Stalemate in Technology: innovation overcome the Depression*, (Massachusetts: Ballinger Publishing Company, 1979).

Miles, T.R., "Gestalt Theory," in The Encyclopedia of Philosophy, New York: Macmillan Publishing Co., vols. 3 and 4, 1967.

Mishan, Edward Joshua, *Cost-Benefit Analysis,* 4th Ed. London: Unwin Hyman, 1988.

Moran, Michael. "New England Transcendentalism," in The Encyclopedia of Philosophy, (New York: Macmillan Publishing Co., Vols. 3 and 4, 1967).

Mundell, Robert A. , "Growth, Stability, and Inflationary Finance," Journal *of Political Economy*, 73, 1963.

Pindyck, R.S., and Rubinfeld, D.L., *Econometric Models and Econometric*, 2nd ed., New York: McGraw-Hills, 1981.

Ott, J. Steven, *The Organizational Culture Perspectives*, (Pacific Grove, California: Brooks/Cole Publishing Company, 1989).

Quirk, James and Saposnik, Rubin, *Introduction to General Equilibrium Theory and Welfare Economics*, New York: McGraw-Hill, 1968.

Rima, Ingrid, *Development of Economic Analysis*, 7th ed., New York: Routledge, 2009.

Rodinson, M., *Islam and Capitalism*, Trans. B. Pearce, Austin: University of Texas, 1981.

Rosenberg, Nathan, Technology *and American Economic Growth*, New York: M. E. Sharp, 1972.

Ruttan, V. W. , "Usher and Schumpeter on Invention, and Technological Change," Quarterly *Journal of Economics*, 1960, 602.

Ruttan, Vernon W. , "Usher and Schumpeter on Invention, Innovation, and Technological change," Quarterly *Journal of Economics*, 1960, 73.

Samuelson, Anthony Paul. Economics, 11th Ed., New York: McGraw-Hill, 1980.

Savich, R.S., and Thomson, L. A., *Resource Allocation within the Product Life Cycles*, Business Topic, MSU: MSU, fall 1978.

Schmooker, Jacob, *Invention and Economic Growth*, Massachusetts: Harvard University Press, 1966.

Schultz, Theodore W. , *Investing in People: The Economics of Population Quality*, Berkley: University of California Press, 1982.

Schumpeter, Joseph A., *Business Cycles*, vol. 1. New York: McGraw Hill Book Company, 1939.

—. *Business Cycles: A Theoretical, Historical, and Statistical Analysis of the Capitalists Process,* vol. I, New York: McGraw Hill Book Company, 1938.

—. *The Theory of Economic Development: An Inquiry into Profits, Capital, Credit, Interest, and Business Cycle*, Trans., Redvers Opie, London: Oxford University Press, Reprint 1980.

Smith, Adam., *An Inquiry into the Nature and Cause of Wealth of Nations*, Edited by E. Cannon, Chicago: University of Chicago Press, 1976.

—. *An Inquiry into the Nature and Causes of Wealth of Nations*, vol. 2, 2nd ed., Oxford: the Clarendon Press, 1988.

—. *The Theory of Moral Sentiments*, London, 1st ed., 1757.

Smith, E.J. Chambers, R.H. Scott and R.S., *National Income Analysis and Forecasting*, Glenview: Scott, Foresman and Company, 1975.

Spiegle, Henry William., *The Growth of Economic thought*, North Carolina: Duke University Press, 1983.

Stigler, George J., *The Theory of Price*, 3rd ed., New York: The Macmillan Company, 1966.

Takaki, Ronald., *A Different Mirror: A History of Multicultural America*, London: Little Brown and Company, 1993.

Taylor, John R., *An Introduction to Error Analysis*, Mill Valley: University Science Books, 1982.

Thirtle, Colin G. and Ruttan V. W., *The Role of Demand and Supply in the Generation of Diffusion of Technological Change*, Switzerland, 1987.

U. S. President, *Economic Report of the President*, (Washington, D.C.: Government printing office, 1990)

Usher, Abbot Payson, *A History of Mechanical Inventions*, London: Oxford University Press, 1954.

Usher, Abbot Payson, *A History of Mechanical Inventions,* Revised ed., London: Oxford University Press, 1954.

Viner, Jacob, *Studies in the Theories of International Trade*, New York: Harper and Brothers publishers, 1937.

Wainwright, A. C. Chiang and K., *Fundamental Methods of Mathematical Economics*, 4th ed., Boston: McGraw-Hill Irwin, 2005.

Webster, Merriam, *Merriam-Webster's Collegiate Dictionary*, 9th ed., Springfield: M.W. Inc., 1985.

Young, Hugh D., *Statistical Treatment of Experimental Data*, New York: McGraw-Hill, 1962.

<u>FERDAT, AND LEGALS</u>

FAKHRAIE EDUCATION RESEARCH
DEVELOPMENT AND TRUST

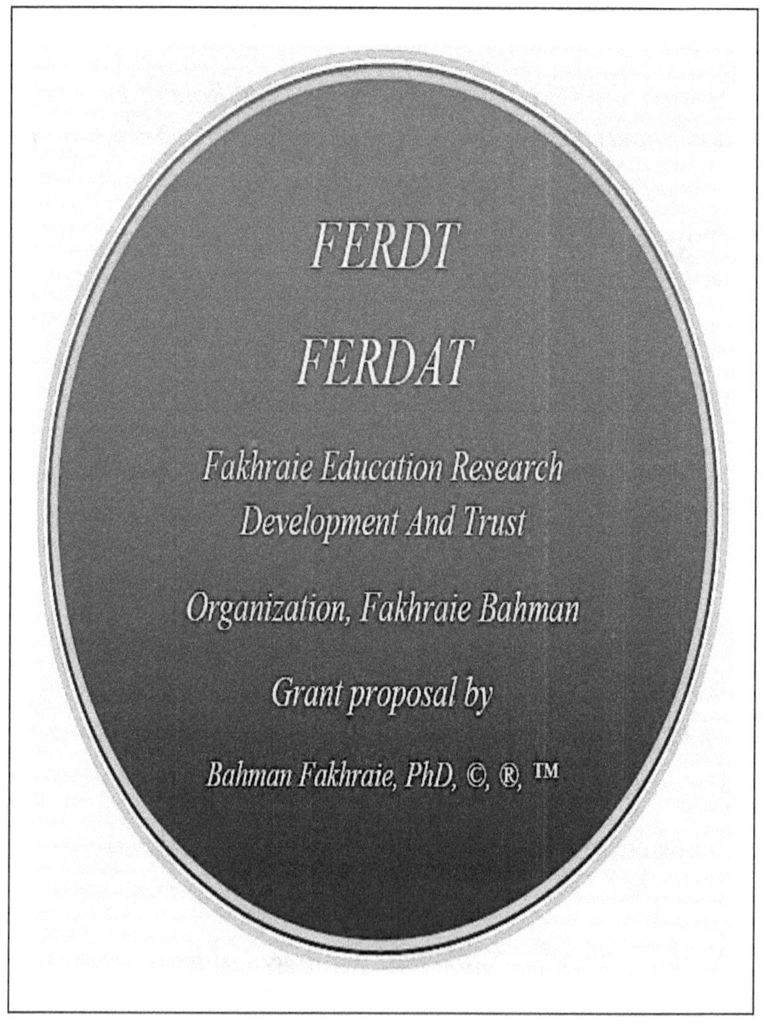

FERDT
FERDAT
Fakhraie Education Research
Development And Trust
Organization, Fakhraie Bahman
Grant proposal by
Bahman Fakhraie, PhD, ©, ®, ™

Budgetary, Managerial Directive and Legal Clauses

Legal letter and charges for unauthorized information use.

Section 1, Mission Statement

Section 2, Budgetary Clause

Section 3, Managerial Clause

Section 4, Legal Clause

Section 5, Organization Chart

Section 6, Data Management

Section 7, Vita

Legal letter is in cases of e-fraud, misuse of firms' information, or harm under sec. G. All linked and relaying entities, institutions, governmental agencies are accountable no exception.

Dear Sirs, persons, INC., (illegal use of firms' info), your current bill is **$10,000, ≤Ceiling $60 mils.** On behalf of Dr. Bahman Fakhraie, FERDAT, and the firm, family trusts.

These are the current charges related to illegal e-fraud and all harmful misuse of firms information, after the first time we asked you to terminate all contract and remove our name, firms' name etc. on this date.

1-Illegal use, the unapproved initial use of firm's name, contact name, duns #, any and all information supplied to USA government for the sole purpose of firm doing business with USA government, grant.gov, and NSF, Universities, other governmental and tribal entities, and all grantors. Minimum charges are $10,000.00, up to the ceiling of $ 60 million.

2-Use of firm contacts, names, address phone #, TIN/#s, and any information related to that.

Minimum charges are $10,000.00, up to the ceiling of $60 mils.

3- Continuation after repeated formal request to terminate illegal actions, sending junk e-mail, junk mail, forcing this firm to send back, by mail and certified mail. Legal costs related to that.

Minimum charges are $10,000.00 per each event, up to the ceiling of $60 mils.

4- Interference with firm soul business, time sensitive writing of government and private grants, at grant.gov, and NSF, universities, private foundations, NGOs and all grantors, with 4.5 million dollars floor. The Minimum charges are 4.5 million dollars, up to the ceiling of $60 mils.

4- Absolute or required non-disclosures by the firm or Dr. Fakhraie will require pre-paid plan with minimum flooring pay. Flex-legalism targeted at the firm, or Dr. B. Fakhraie will be due cause for nonpaid termination by the same, and harm-terms of Sec G of private contracts.

6- Punitive damages are up to 60 million dollars, if you do not stop, after the first notification.

Please make an effort to pay your bill. There will be additional charges added and sent to you for each time you try to contact the same entities, after the same dated termination notices.

Dr. BF, this is part of the legal notices under sec G, or formal termination notice dates.

Section 1, Mission Statement

To formulate optimum functionality in management teams, in order to make profitable and beneficial contributions, and create opportunity for merited advancements, to advance research in my fields of study. Utilizing rare combination of theory and empiricism, cultivated in multi-cultural inclusive settings in academic and private enterprises, I enhance the management in productivity and completion of productive projects, or suggest corrective recursive evaluation and total quality control improvements.

Experiences, among fields of International Trade, Managerial, and Production theories in Economics, Finance, Personal Finance management, and Businesses, which modern business and academic institutions find very expensive to employ and too costly not to employ. My extensive backgrounds help me advance research in my fields of study.

Section 2, Budgetary Clause

* All initial dedicated deposits (inflows) will be transferred to a FREDT, or FREDAT business account.

* No allotments or contracts activity will take place, until full transfer of funds has taken place per contracts. The cash-accounting method is used for tax purposes.
* Alteration to submit to requirements and regulations will fully transfer all risks, fees, and penalties, and legal responsibilities, to the source of the requirements.

* There will be a minimum product list, or writing, or proposal-output for further research, which will be presented and agreed to at the initial phases.
* This will be the only output legally required at the end of contract, or at the end of grant periods.
* There is a managerial flow chart enclosed to enhance comprehensions of cash flow, read after the legal notes section.

Section 3, Managerial Clause

* Dr. Bahman Fakhraie will act as agent, manger, and soul administrator, Executives director, Principle Investigator PI for FERDT, FERDAT, Fakhraie Bahman Organization, with full rights to take legal action and make final settlement on its accounts.
* Dr. Bahman Fakhraie will act as agent, manger, and soul administrator for Fakhraie Bahman Organization, with full right to take legal action on its accounts.
* A general electronic bookkeeping is followed, on periodical bases, as grants require it. Current standard is quarterly, post full disbursements of grant funding. (FRR is required quarterly)
* Details, information, managerial technologies are legally protected, and no such disclosure will be made of the Organization, administrator, assignees, or representatives of FERDT, FERDAT, or Fakhraie Bahman Organization. All copyright materials are

marketable, or further developed by Mr. Fakhraie. All existing rights are reserved.

* All informal and formal requests can be made by mail, or email.
* There is forfeiture of all advances, in cases of mortality, health, or attempt at disbarment, legal action, harm, against soul administrator, Fakhraie Bahman Organization, with full right to take legal action on its accounts.
* Any and all such request will have to forward additional funding for legal representations and undue imposition of costs or harm, please read the legal note and sec. G. It will always apply.
* Alteration to submit to requirements and regulations will fully transfer all risks, fees, and penalties, and legal responsibilities, to the source of the requirements.

* The reviewers will have access to a portion of the progress.
* Full transparencies are practiced for authorized agents only, mostly through the internet, after proper signatures are obtained.
* All future development, educational development will have to be contracted, or signed out temporarily.
* All copyrights and proprietary rights are reserved, granted, accorded to Dr. Bahman Fakhraie, and his living trust.
* The final product in initial agreement will be shared with the grantors, after all the financial settlements have been met.

* PI, FERDAT; Dr. Fakhraie, Bahman

Dr. Bahman Fakhraie, PhD, UOU, UT, USA

* Position Classification, Executive level I,
* Salary exceeds Fed Cap for private contracts.
* NSF ID, 000586796, Organizational ID Code, P 269878425
* Private for Profit Business:
* DUNS Number D&B # [redacted]89684,
* CAGE/NCAGE: [redacted]S3, Congressional Districts, UT_001
* Sec G of private contract always applies
* For other institutional DUNS, etc. Please, check cover letter, or contact PI. Thanks

* PI Information(dated)

Grantors information goes here

Section 4, Legal Clause, All Right Reserved & Other Legal Notes

All rights will revert to author after 3 years, if limited rights are contracted.

E. Speech, Lecture Tours, and Research Papers & Follow Up:

All publications or Grant-products are commonly published on completion, USA Library of Congress, Trade Journals, Or Author's websites, etc.

Contact for individualized contracts

F. for Time Donation, And Charity Events: 1. 5% of Net contracts paid 2. Time by Appointments Only.3. Write Donations Checks to Fakhraie Trust fund / Bahman Fakhraie

G. Any and All Risks or Harms invokes these legal clauses. The Following legal clauses are base minimum, and will not limit all rights and legal protection, with uniform constitutional rights they are implied and accorded. Contractually all rights are implied and accorded. Please, read all the legal notes before using any materials.

G1. In Cases of misuse of these materials, plagiarisms, use to put at risk of harm, or to harm, (Legal, or Etc.) the firm, CEO, FERDT, president: Mr. Bahman Fakhraie, His family members, it will result in $60 million legal action per each event in United States Courts/ any Jurisdictions determined or set by author or a trust set up by Mr. Bahman Fakhraie. Also, use of creative ideas and intellectual properties for any commerce direct or indirect or by proxy, expansions of outlines, attempts to defraud, over charge, harm with illegal acts, misuse of private and confidential materials, information, and properties, letters, checks, e-mails, faxes, any and all communications, and any electronically stored materials and pictures, or false claims against the above entities will be an agreement with and subject to all elements of this contract, and as a user license, without nullifying further and ensuing legal actions or collections, or as directed by the same or authorities. All other contracts are one time contracts and s. t. this contract. Please, notify firm, Mr. Bahman Fakhraie, of all infractions, transactions, or transfer to individuals or to private or government entities in accord with current laws.

G2a. All Costs due to inquiries, related or required business licenses, legal paper works, and hours, all costs related to corrective or reparation publicity, bonding and insurances costs, stock related activities, all costs related to any harm (financial & legal) will be charges to the sources and inquirers, and none to the firm or Bahman Fakhraie, his family, or any and all of their related assets. All attempts to harm, engagements, cashing checks or accepting cash from the same entities is an agreement with all elements of this contract.

G2b. All copy rights associated with written works and further development of all works remains with the author Bahman Fakhraie or his trusts. All development rights are reserved by the same entities.

G3. Any and all unsolicited commercial phone calls, to Mr. Bahman Fakhraie and, his family will result to a minimum of $ 500 per call charged to the source, due and payable in the same month the call is made, all other elements of this contract also apply, all contracts remain subservient to this contract, all costs of collection and legal actions also are added to the bill payable by source and not Bahman Fakhraie and these entities.

G4.All Consultation and coaching involves risks due to market, business, political, etc. costs and damages related to all such risk are paid by individuals or business entities involved and none is implied or taken by Bahman Fakhraie, his family, or any related assets, under any and all conditions. These entities' court fees are $10,000; et minimum.

G5.Uncomfortable conditions, misapplications of any law to harm, harassment, odd-hour calls, etc will be due cause for termination of services without refund, and are actionable per this contract.

§§§§

All Right Reserved & Other Legal Notes

All publications or Grant-products are published on completion, USA Library of Congress, Trade Journals, Or Author's websites, etc. All rights revert to author after 3 years, if limited rights are contracted.

E. Speech, Lecture Tours, Research Papers & Follow Up:

1. Per Each Event-$ 350,000 +.

2. with Foreign Travel-$ 3,000,000

3. Book/Cash Advance floor Min; Net Royalties ~40%

4. Scripts: /Starting from.....................$ 300,000

5. Movie Script (120+Pages).................$ 3,000,000

6. Or Cash Advance Plus 2% of All Gross paid annually

7. Consultations Fee/Initial charge non-refunded $ 10,000, & ...10 %

8. Business limited ventures, partnerships, etc. .... ≥ 30%

9. Salary executive level I

F. for Time Donation, And Charity Events: 1. 5% of Net contracts paid 2. Time by Appointments Only.3. Write Donations Checks to Fakhraie Trust fund / Bahman Fakhraie. G. Any and All Risks or Harms invokes these legal clauses. The Following legal clauses are base minimum, and will not limit all rights and legal protection, with uniform constitutional rights they are implied and accorded. Contractually all rights are implied and accorded. Please, read all the legal notes before using any materials. G1. In Cases of misuse of these materials, plagiarisms, use to put at risk of harm, or to harm, (Legal, or Etc.) the firm, CEO: Mr. Bahman Fakhraie, His family members, will result in $60 million legal action per each event in United States Courts/Jurisdictions determine by author or a trust set up by Mr. Bahman Fakhraie. Also, use of creative ideas intellectual properties, expansions of outlines, attempts to defraud, over charge, harm with illegal acts, misuse of private and confidential materials and properties, letters, e-mails, faxes, any and all communications, and any electronically stored materials and pictures, or false claims against the above entities will be an agreement with all elements of this contract, and as a use license, without nullifying ensuing legal actions or collections, or as directed by the same or authorities. Please, notify firm, Mr. Bahman Fakhraie, of all infractions, transactions, or transfer to individuals or to private or government entities. G2a. All Costs due to inquiries, related or required business licenses, legal paper works and hours, all costs related to corrective or reparation publicity, bonding and insurances costs, stock related activities, all costs related to any harm (financial & legal) will be charges to the sources and inquirers, and none to the firm or Bahman Fakhraie, his family, or any and all of their related assets. All attempts to harm, engagements, cashing checks or accepting cash from the same entities is an agreement with all elements of this contract. G2b. All copy rights associated with written works and further development of all works remains with the author Bahman Fakhraie or his trusts. Any and all development rights are reserved by the same entities. G3. Any and all unsolicited commercial phone calls to Mr. Bahman Fakhraie, his family will result to a minimum of $ 500 per call charged to the source, due and payable in the same month the call is made, all other elements of this contract also apply, all contracts remain subservient to this contract, all costs of collection and legal actions also are added to the bill payable by source and not Bahman Fakhraie and these entities. G4.All Consultation and coaching involves risks due to market, business, political, etc. costs and damages related to all such risk are paid by individuals or business entities involved and none is implied or taken by Bahman Fakhraie, his family, or any related assets, under any and all conditions. These entities' court fees are $10,000; et minimum. G5.Uncomfortable conditions, misapplications of any law to harm, harassment, odd-hour calls, etc. will be due cause for termination of services without refund, and are actionable per this contract.

§§§§

Letter of Agreement with FRDET and Fakhraie Bahman

I/We (Ms., Mrs., Mr.):

....

Business Name:

....

Social Security numbers: ....../......./............ ..../......./...............

Tax ID Numbers: ....

Driver License Numbers:

....

Passport (Birth Certificate) Numbers:

....

Have read all the information supplied by Dr. Bahman Fakhraie, and /or FRDET (Trust, LLP). Agree to supply all correct financial and related information and select the following services by marking (X), or Letter a b c, Or Number 1 2 3, or write and specify. Agree to the power of attorney required to confirm or acquire financial and related information. Plus a check for $3000, for preliminary registrations, legal and financial inquiries, and licensing fees.

1: □ 2: □ 3: □ 4: □ 5: □ 6: □ 7: □ 8: □

Specify which kinds of the following accounts you will require:

Individual/Gov. □ Joints □ Joint with survival rights □ Trusts □

Details: ....

Business types:

Ltd Partnership (LLP, LLC) □ Soul Owner □

Teconomics of Budget Ethics

Inc/Gov □ Firm □

Details: ....

I/We agree to pay the fees and costs as they accrue, after 30 days a charge of %10 per annum is added to past due amounts until they are settled or paid in full. That at least 75% charges and expenses are paid no later than six month after initial reports or outlines are examined. That all travel lodgings and phone charges, legal research, and research hours, I/We request are fully paid. I/We have read and understand the nature of business, business cycles, market price fluctuation risks, currency fluctuation risks, social and political risks, natural and climatic risks, and all other risks herewith not itemized; therefore, I/we accept all financial losses, responsibilities, all punitive or compensatory damages that occur for all activities that are undertaken based on or claimed related to the report or reports, advise and etc., generated by Money Wise Firm, Bahman Fakhraie or all the entities named, agents, and associates. I/We understand in cases of any false, misleading, or withholding information the Money Wise Firm and all entities named above will not be held accountable, responsible, financially or otherwise, and will be refunded for any damages fully. I/We release all others associated with Money Wise Firm, and Bahman Fakhraie from financial losses, responsibilities, all compensatory and punitive charges concerning activities I/We undertake.

Sign (full name, titles, and address)

Business (Name, Address; Agents' title):

Section 5, Organization Chart

⇔Requests for grants, grant and contract proposals

and Minimums contracted output Grant Funds,

⇓ Organization DUNS, University DUNS ⇓

Administrator ⇒FRDAT

⇓

FERDAT & FERDAT- C

Publishing and Production

President, Administrator, Executive level 1

⇓

Tasks and controls, TQC, and Redo, Recycles

⇔Tax and expense disbursements

⇓

Completed project Vs. Minimums contracted output

⇔ Informal notification of source of funds, with future project proposal if any,

⇒Formal and final notification from FRDET, FERDAT

⇔ Final confirmation of conclusion from Administrators

⇒ Final confirmation of conclusion from Organization Fakhraie

⇔ Keeping communication and network open to future project.

Section 6, DATA MANAGEMENT:

Relevant data will be managed, and stored. Moreover, the data and the progression of data used will be stored post completion. As a common practice, Dr. Bahman Fakhraie will, also preserve a historical over view of data for legal purposes, for future use. A portion of that will be shared if requested in written form, post settlement of all expenses. The ethical requirements will be followed in accordance with the applied law established.

The final product will be shared with the grantors, after all the financial settlements have been met. The reviewers will have access to a portion of the progress. All publications or Grant-products are published on completion for academic and educational research, USA Library of Congress, trade journals, FERDAT

Publishing, author's websites, other academic journals, etc.

All rights will revert to author after 3 years, if contract exits for limited rights.

Labor laws and benefit distribution will be according to the institutional Fed Cap limits, private contracts; vendors are responsible for their own legal obligations. (Publication Ink, FedExx, kinkcos, vendors etc.)

CPA and Legal establishment, outside to this entity will be contracted to handle more complex issues when they arise, all cost are due, prior to any such required actions are requested.

Full transparencies are practiced for authorized agents only, mostly through the internet, after proper signatures are obtained. All copyrights and proprietary rights are granted, accorded and reserved to Dr. Bahman Fakhraie,

All future development, educational development will have to be contracted, or signed out temporarily, they will revert to Dr. Bahman Fakhraie, in case of all legal issues.

These and other clauses will be amended and upgraded as required over time, they all apply.

Absolut or required non-disclosures by the firm or Dr. Fakhraie will require pre-paid plan with minimum flooring pay. Flex-legalism targeted at the firm, or Dr. B. Fakhraie will be due cause for nonpaid termination by the same.

G. Any and All Risks or Harms invokes these legal clauses. The Following legal clauses are base minimum, and will not limit all rights and legal protection, with uniform constitutional rights they are implied and accorded. Contractually all rights are implied and accorded. Please, read all the legal notes before using any materials.

Sec 7, Check CURRICULUM VITA

BOOK PROMOTIONS

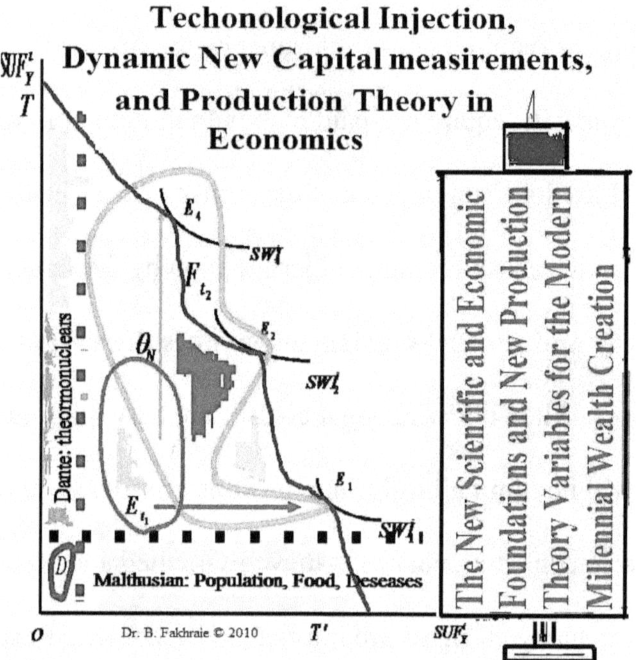

Dr. Bahman Fakhraie's books web page link, Books web page at, http://bahfecon.wix.com/bahfecon, Author books, http://www.amazon.com/Dr.-Bahman-Fakhraie/e/B00IKAR1CM/ref=ntt_athr_dp_pel_1

DEMAND & SUPPLY SIDES OF TECHNOLOGICAL INJECTIONS

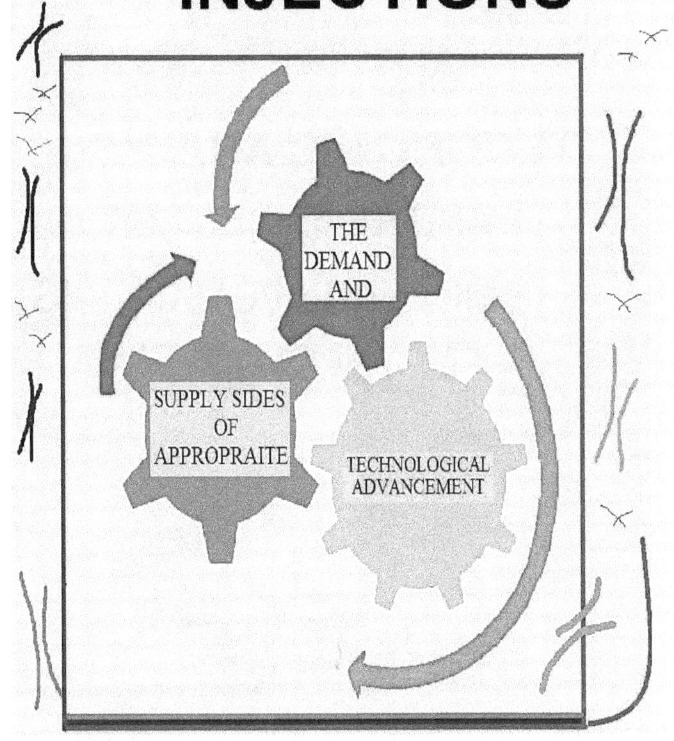

Dr. Bahman Fakhraie's books web page link,
http://bahfecon.wix.com/bahfecon

Book link, *https://www.createspace.com/4187823*

TECONOMICS

OF

OF

Bahman Fakhraie, Ph.D.

https://www.createspace.com/4121720

TECONOMICS

OF

DYNAMIC SUSTAINABLE

BUDGETS

Dynamic Sustainable Modular Production Budgets

X

Bahman Fakhraie, Ph.D.

https://www.createspace.com/4536462?ref=1147694&utm_id=6026

TREATISE ON TECONOMICS ØF DYNAMIC RISKS

ALL NATURAL DISASTERS,

&

ENERGY RESOURCES PRODCUTION DISASTERS

Bahman Fakhraie, Ph.D.

https://www.createspace.com/4187823

EBook, http://www.amazon.com/POLITICAL-MONOPOLISTIC-CAPITALISM-

WEALTH-CONCENTRATION-ebook/dp/B00HQPBZBK/ref=sr_1_1/180-8302534-5503723?s=digital-text&ie=UTF8&qid=1389203920&sr=1-1#reader_B00HQPBZBK

Print Books link, ***http://bahfecon.wix.com/bahfecon***

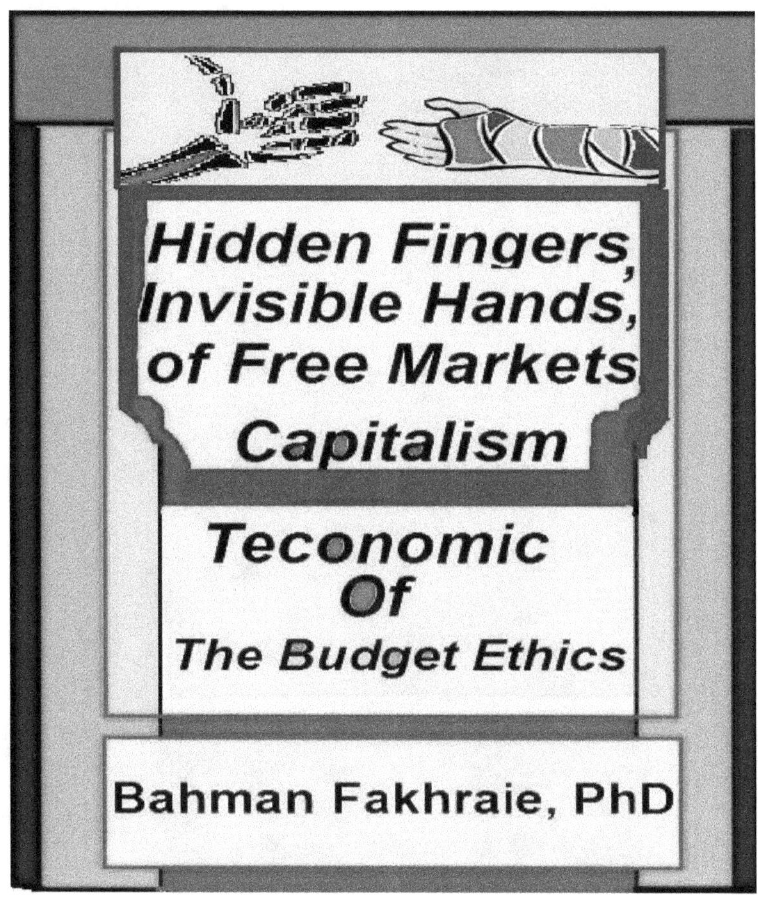

Hidden Fingers,
Invisible Hands,
of Free Markets
Capitalism
Teconomic
Of
The Budget Ethics
Bahman Fakhraie, PhD

Dr. Bahman Fakhraie's books,

, ***http://bahfecon.wix.com/bahfecon***

, http://www.amazon.com/Dr.-Bahman-Fakhraie/e/B00IKAR1CM/ref=ntt_athr_dp_ pel_1

To All Lives

Dr. Bahman Fakhraie, PhD in Economics, University of Utah, and his dissertation added to the influences of the Unorthodox Holistic Economic doctrine and complemented the modern orthodox economic theories, in the millennial age of technological paradigm shifts. He applies analytical skills with gestalt study of history, mathematics, and econometrics to economic analysis, with scientific background. He is a Published Economist, Author, Researcher, Investor, and Private Contractor. His skills are in international trade and finance, economic production (theory and application), growth and development theory, econometrics, agriculture economics, and agronomy. These are greatly valued skills combinations to employ.

Books links, http://bahfecon.wix.com/bahfecon

Book- ISBN-10:0989453936,
ISBN-13:978-0-9894539-3-6